"There is a great deal of attention currently being [...] relating to mental health and stress in [...] the mistake of thinking that th[...] a cluttered sector of anecdotes, [...] Putwain's contribution is learned [...] interesting read. More important [...] and thoughtful contribution from [...] substantial background in the area. It explores [...], prevalence, and impact of high exam stress, and the [...] shows how this issue can be managed to improve the experience and outcomes of this group of students. An example of an area that most will find interesting is dealing with the often-cited belief that 'a little bit of stress is a good thing', whilst not denying some partial truth in this notion the author explores it in revealing ways and then goes on to show what this means for classroom practice. An accessible academic book that explores a very topical misunderstood and misrepresented area, that also gives practical suggestions for applying the findings, this is well worth reading and seeing what gains you can take from it. As the leader of an outstanding Sixth Form College that has been at the forefront of adopting lessons from cognitive science for many years, I found this book to be thought provoking and will take lessons learnt from it to inform some of our future teaching and curriculum developments."

Mike Kilbride, *Principal, Birkenhead 6th Form College, and CEO BePART Trust*

"Whilst taking exams may be a part of life, experiencing exam anxiety doesn't need to be! Drawing on theory and research, this authoritative book provides plenty of practical suggestions for identifying and supporting students with exam anxiety. A must-read for anyone working with students anxious about exams."

Wendy Symes, *Research Fellow, University of Hamburg*

UNDERSTANDING AND HELPING TO OVERCOME EXAM ANXIETY

This important book considers what we know about test and exam anxiety, including how it is defined, its characteristics, how it can be identified, why and how it develops, and what can be done to support test-anxious students.

Addressing the pressures of preparing for and taking high-stakes tests and exams in many educational systems throughout the world, the book offers additional steps that schools, policymakers, and parents can take to further reduce test anxiety. Looking at the science and providing readers with an accessible framework of facts and no-nonsense details, the book addresses the most frequently asked questions and topics, including the difference between exam stress and exam anxiety, the signs and indicators of exam anxiety, and the consequences of exam anxiety on educational achievement. Former teacher and current Professor and leading authority on exam anxiety, David Putwain includes a chapter explaining psychological interventions for test anxiety, specifically STEPS, an intervention designed to help professionals identify and support highly test-anxious students.

Putwain's book is essential reading for teachers, school leaders, parents, and professionals involved in school welfare. It may also be of interest to counsellors, government education departments, and examining bodies.

David Putwain is Professor of Education at Liverpool John Moores University, UK. His research interests focus on the motivations and emotions that arise in achievement settings and how these impact, and are in turn impacted by, achievement, well-being, and mental health. David has been researching test and exam anxiety for over 20 years.

BPS ASK THE EXPERTS IN PSYCHOLOGY SERIES

British Psychological Society

Routledge, in partnership with the British Psychological Society (BPS), is pleased to present BPS Ask the Experts, a new popular science series that addresses key issues and answers the burning questions. Drawing on the expertise of established psychologists, every book in the series provides authoritative and straightforward guidance on pressing topics that matter to real people in their everyday lives.

All books in the BPS Ask the Experts series are written for the reader with no prior knowledge or experience. For answers to everything you ever wanted to know about issues important to you, ask the expert!

Managing Your Gaming and Social Media Habits
From Science to Solutions
Catherine Knibbs

How to Live Well with Dementia
Expert Help for People Living with Dementia and their Family, Friends, and Care Partners
Anthea Innes, Megan E O'Connell, Carmel Geoghegan, and Phyllis Fehr

Understanding and Helping to Overcome Exam Anxiety
What Is It, Why Is It Important and Where Does It Come From?
David Putwain

For more information about this series, please visit: BPS Ask The Experts in Psychology Series – Book Series – Routledge & CRC Press

UNDERSTANDING AND HELPING TO OVERCOME EXAM ANXIETY

WHAT IS IT, WHY IS IT IMPORTANT AND WHERE DOES IT COME FROM?

DAVID PUTWAIN

LONDON AND NEW YORK

Cover image: © jayk7/Getty Images

First published 2025
by Routledge
4 Park Square, Milton Park, Abingdon, Oxon OX14 4RN

and by Routledge
605 Third Avenue, New York, NY 10158

Routledge is an imprint of the Taylor & Francis Group, an informa business

© 2025 David Putwain

The right of David Putwain to be identified as author of this work has been asserted in accordance with sections 77 and 78 of the Copyright, Designs and Patents Act 1988.

All rights reserved. No part of this book may be reprinted or reproduced or utilised in any form or by any electronic, mechanical, or other means, now known or hereafter invented, including photocopying and recording, or in any information storage or retrieval system, without permission in writing from the publishers.

Trademark notice: Product or corporate names may be trademarks or registered trademarks, and are used only for identification and explanation without intent to infringe.

British Library Cataloguing-in-Publication Data
A catalogue record for this book is available from the British Library

ISBN: 9781032716381 (hbk)
ISBN: 9781032713335 (pbk)
ISBN: 9781032716411 (ebk)

DOI: 10.4324/9781032716411

Typeset in Bembo
by codeMantra

Access the Support Material: routledge.com/9781032713335

In memory of Vicky Buddug Putwain
1942–2022

CONTENTS

Who Am I and Why Am I Giving You This Advice?		xiii
Acknowledgements		xvii
1	What Is Exam Anxiety (and What Is It Not)?	1
2	How Prevalent Is Exam Anxiety?	19
3	What Are the Consequences of High Exam Anxiety for Educational Achievement?	41
4	How Does Exam Anxiety Relate to Mental Health and Well-Being?	69
5	How Does Exam Anxiety Arise: Where Does It Come From?	89
6	Interventions for Exam Anxiety: What Can Be Done About It	111
7	Educational Policy: What Does the Future Hold?	141

Glossary	157
Further Reading	163
References	167

WHO AM I AND WHY AM I GIVING YOU THIS ADVICE?

After completing an undergraduate degree in Psychology, and training as a teacher, I worked in schools and sixth-form colleges for the next 12 years mainly teaching GCSE and A Level Psychology. In addition, I contributed to GCSE Sociology and Statistics. During this period, I co-authored several A Level Psychology textbooks and revision guides, was an A Level Psychology examiner for the Associated Examination Board (which became part of what is now known as the Assessment and Qualifications Alliance), and subsequently a Principal Examiner for the Edexcel Foundation (now Pearson Edexcel). I was part of the group that designed the first Psychology A Level Specification for Edexcel, for the Curriculum 2000 reform of A Level examinations.

While working as a teacher, I completed a master's degree in Applied Psychology and a PhD into the anxiety and stress experienced by students in Key Stage 4 (Years 10 and 11) as they studied for, and took, high-stakes secondary school exit examinations (GCSEs). On completing my PhD, I moved to Edge Hill University where I worked initially in the Department of Social and Psychological Sciences and founded an undergraduate degree in Educational Psychology in 2009. In 2013, I was promoted to Reader of Psychology and in 2014 joined the Faculty of Education where I was promoted to Professor of Education. In 2016, I moved to Liverpool John Moores University where I joined the School of Education as a Professor of Education and Early Childhood. I have now supervised 14 doctoral students to completion and must be one of only a handful of people who have taught psychology at all levels from GCSE through to doctoral level.

I have been a member of the British Psychology Society since 1994, became a Chartered Psychologist in 2006, an Associate Fellow of the Society in 2013, and a Fellow of the Society in 2018. I joined the Psychology of Education Section of the British Psychology Society in 2006, joined the committee of the Section in 2011, and was Chair of the Section from 2012 to 2018. I have organised, or co-organised the annual conference of the Section in 2015, 2019, 2021, 2022, and 2023. I have been an Associate Editor of some of the leading journals in the field of educational psychology, including *Learning and Individual Differences*, *Educational Psychology*, and the *British Journal of Educational Psychology*. I presently sit on the Editorial Boards of Learning and Instruction, Educational Psychology, and the Social Psychology of Education, and am the co-Editor-in-Chief of the *British Journal of Educational Psychology*.

The research programme I started with doctoral studies into the stress and anxiety experienced by students preparing for, and taking, GCSEs continues to this day. It has been expanded to include students of all ages, although I do have a particular focus on students aged 14–19 years taking GCSEs and A Levels. I also study other emotions (both positive and negative) in relation to learning, classroom, and testing experiences, student motivation, engagement, well-being, and mental health. I have published this work in over 130 peer-reviewed journal articles and book chapters. My approach is that research in education and educational psychology must have a practical and applied focus; it must be of benefit to students, teachers, schools, and the wider education system. If research findings are of no practical use, they are developing new knowledge for its own sake. However, for research findings to be useful in more than one context, it must have a strong theoretical basis, and for research findings to be trusted, they have to be conducted in an open, transparent, and rigorous fashion. These goals (practical use, application, theory, and rigour) are not mutually exclusive.

Others, including readers of this book, will be the judge of whether my research programme have achieved these goals or not. I am particularly pleased when research findings have a positive impact on students. Some brief examples include the Office of Qualifications and Examinations Regulation (Ofqual) publishing and making widely available my brief essential advice for students on dealing with exam pressures. Government education and school ministers reversed their proposed decision to abolish formulae sheets for GCSE mathematics and physics in 2022 on the basis of my research findings. Finally, I have developed with colleagues a brief, evidence-based, low-cost, intervention designed for highly test and exam anxious persons aged 14–18 years. Informal feedback from students, and formal research evaluation, has shown that students are less anxious, less worried, and feel more in control and confident about taking GCSEs and A levels after participating in this intervention. If I have in any way contributed to students being to achieve their potential and experience less distress in doing so, my research endeavours have been worthwhile.

ACKNOWLEDGEMENTS

I would like to express my sincere thanks to all of the colleagues and students I have collaborated with in quest to understand test and exam anxiety and how students experiencing high exam anxiety can be supported. In no particular order, I would like to thank Kevin Woods, Liz Connors, Laura Nicholson, Tony Daly, Suzanne Chamberlain, Shireen Sadreddini, Reinhard Pekrun, Nathaniel von der Embse, Martin Daumiller, Kristina Stockinger, Stephanie Licthenfeld, Christine Roberts, Tahrim Hussain, and Emma Rainbird. Special thanks go to Wendy Symes, who I have not only collaborated on numerous studies with but also kindly provided an extensive review of the draft manuscript for this book. In addition, Nathaniel von der Embse provided an additional review of Chapter 2, and Jerrell Cassady and Addison Helsper of Chapter 3 (especially formulating the critique of the Yerkes-Dodson curve and the visualisation of Figure 3.8). I would also like to acknowledge the British Academy who provided funding for some of the projects described in this book.

1

WHAT IS EXAM ANXIETY (AND WHAT IS IT NOT)?

SETTING THE SCENE

In 2021, the Anna Freud Centre in London published findings from the Healthy School Survey (Cortina et al., 2021). This survey comprised responses from 3,298 11- to 19-year-olds in the UK about the factors contributing to their mental health and well-being. In total, 58.2% said exams had a negative impact on their mental health. Unsurprisingly, the figures were higher for 14–16-year-olds (62.6%) and those aged 16 years and older (61.7%). These are the ages when students are preparing for, and taking, high-stakes school exit exams. These figures were second only to schoolwork, and much higher than family problems (29.8%), bullying (28.6%), discrimination (27.4%), social media (15.1%), and friendships (11.3%).

In response to the question of what teachers should discuss with students in order to support their mental health, 77.1% identified exam stress. Again, the figure was higher for 14–16-year-olds (79.6%) and those aged 16 years and older (81.6%). Exam stress followed depression and anxiety (92.4%), body image (87.1%), identity (86.9%), self-harm (86.2), and eating disorders (81.5%). Exam stress was higher than planning for the future (71.2%), sexual relationships (70.7%), risk-taking (69.3%), puberty (64.8%), peer pressure (63.7%), bereavement (56.8%), and social media (54.6%).

In the 2015 *Programme for International Student Assessment (PISA) survey*, which surveyed 389,215 15-year-old adolescent students from 51 countries, 55.5% of respondents replied agree or strongly agree to the question, "Even if I am well prepared for a test, I feel very anxious". In the UK, this figure was 71.9%. These findings indicate that the pressures associated with tests and exams are something that many students are concerned about and would like support for. When considered against other concerns, tests and exams rank after well-acknowledged mental health risks (anxiety, depression, eating disorders, and self-harm). However, tests and exams also rank above many other issues that arguably receive more attention and support, including bullying, discrimination, and social media. These findings are highly instructive in showing us where the pressures associated with tests and exams sit in the minds of students.

I would argue that the pressures associated with tests and exams are not something that has been widely acknowledged. At least, this is my experience, in the UK, of researching this topic for over 20 years and working as a teacher for years prior to that. Perhaps there has been a slow change over the past decade as young people have been encouraged to voice concerns about their health and well-being. However, it is still an issue that I believe is not given the attention that it deserves. Throughout this book, I will present the case that test and exam anxieties are worthy of our attention because of the potential damage they can do to learning, achievement, well-being, mental health, and, ultimately, one's future. In addition, I will consider steps that can be taken to mitigate test and exam anxiety, and how to support students experiencing high levels of anxiety around tests and exams. One of the most positive findings to come out of the academic literature is that test and exam anxieties are not inevitable and are highly responsive to intervention.

HOW IS EXAM ANXIETY DEFINED?
EXAM ANXIETY AS STATES AND TRAITS

When we are talking and thinking about test or exam anxiety, or indeed any other type of emotional experience, we can refer to a single specific emotional episode over a defined period of time, or we can refer to a general tendency to experience particular emotions in particular settings. For instance, someone may attend a friend's birthday celebration and have a fabulous time for the three hours they were there. Alternatively, one could find a parking space in a crowded parking area and feel a momentary sense of relief at having found a space that might only last for a minute or less. These specific episodes of emotional experiences are referred to by psychologists as 'states'.

Just as persons can experience time-defined experiences of enjoyment and relief, they can also experience specific instances of fear in relation to tests and exams. Such states might be brief and fleeting, perhaps when thinking about an exam that is some distance in the future or when being reminded about a forthcoming exam by a teacher or parent. However, anxiety states could also build in the period immediately prior to an exam and remain intense for the period of that exam before subsiding again.

Nonetheless, some people typically never become anxious about tests, or exams, whereas others typically experience a moderate degree of anxiety, and there are those who consistently become very anxious. When we refer to the general level of anxiety a person experiences about tests or exams, we are referring to what psychologists call 'trait' anxiety. Persons high in trait test anxiety will, give or take, experience high levels of state anxiety in most, if not all, tests and exams. Persons low in trait test anxiety will, give or take, experience low levels of state anxiety in tests and exams.

When defining test anxiety, therefore, it is important to be clear whether we are referring to a single, isolated episode (a state), or the general tendency (the trait). In research studies, it can be useful to look at triggers and outcomes for single episodes of anxiety as well as the general tendency to experience anxiety. For practitioners, however, who may wish to identify students for additional support, intervention, or exam accommodations, or to evaluate the effectiveness of an intervention, it may be more useful to look at the general tendency to experience test or exam anxiety.

An important point to make is that while the enduring tendency to become highly anxious around tests and exams is referred to as a trait, this does not imply that it will not change or be responsive to intervention. The term 'trait' in psychology has also been used for enduring dimensions of personality that are rooted in temperament and largely hard-wired, meaning they are highly stable. While persons may have a typical level of test and exam anxiety, studies have shown that test anxiety does change and, as we will see in Chapter 6, is fortunately responsive to intervention.

ANXIETY AS A REACTION TO PERCEIVED THREAT

What exactly is it that triggers anxiety in test and exam situations? According to Charles Spielberger, one of the psychologists who pioneered work into understanding anxiety, anxiety arises from the perception of a threat. Threats are something that pose a risk, danger, or injury, to our health or well-being. Some people find physical threats (e.g., wild animals or heights) particularly threatening, and hence respond with more elevated anxiety than people who do not find physical threats so threatening. Other people, for example, find social situations threatening, worried that they will embarrass or humiliate themselves, and hence respond with elevated anxiety. Persons who do not find social situations threatening do not respond with elevated anxiety.

The threat associated with social situations is not physical. Even if one is embarrassed, there is no likelihood of a broken leg that might result from a vehicle accident or an impaired respiratory system resulting from a viral infection. The threat of social situations is psychological: how we judge and evaluate ourselves. Psychological threats have variously been described as a possible danger to our sense of self-worth, our self-esteem, or our self-identity. Spielberger, as long ago as 1966, described these different types of psychological threat as 'ego' threat.

Test and exam anxiety is another instance of ego threat. That is the psychological threat posed by an evaluative-performance situation. A performance-evaluative situation is simply one where our performance is assessed, rated, judged, or valued in some way. The threat posed by performance-evaluative situations overlaps to some degree with the threat posed by social situations. Performance-evaluative situations often take place in situations where others are present (e.g., other students taking the exam and the person(s) invigilating or supervising the exam) and the results arising from these situations can be known publicly. However, the main distinction between test and exam anxiety and social anxiety is that with the former, threat is posed by the judgement of academic, rather than social, competence.

Some performance-evaluative situations take the form of presentations, oral examinations, skills tests (like a driving test), or structured clinical evaluations (often used in examinations for medical students with real or simulated patients), where the examiner is present. These situations present threats to one's academic and social competence, and hence, may be especially anxiety-provoking for some persons.

The threat specifically posed by performance-evaluative situations is the possibility of failure and its consequences. Failure could, for instance, result in negative self-judgements of one's ability (e.g., "I am not very clever"), one's expectations (e.g., "I have let my self down"), or one's sense of self-worth (e.g., "I am hopeless"). Failure will be particularly damaging for students who strongly identify as academic or who have strongly internalised academic competence as a basis for their self-esteem. It must be emphasised that failure is highly subjective. What constitutes failure can differ from one student to the next.

For some students, anything other than the highest grade in every subject represents a failure. One student, for instance, told me in an interview some years back:

> In my last history one [exam] in the Year 10 exams I screwed up in that one completely. I know this sounds stupid and people say that I'm being ungrateful but I got a B for it in the end because I messed up on it so much. It's just horrible.
>
> (Putwain, 2009)

For readers unfamiliar with the English grading system at the time (the country where these interviews were conducted), the highest grade was a grade A*, the next grade was A, the next was a B, and C was the official pass grade. This student had achieved one grade higher than a pass but was clearly disappointed. For other students, failure would not be meeting a target grade (either self-generated or provided by others) or not attaining a minimum pass grade.

Students can also worry about being judged negatively by people who are important to them and/ or whose approval they seek and negative judgement they wish to avoid (e.g., parents, other family members, peers, teachers, and so on). Consider, for instance, this student,

> People think if you don't do well at school you're rubbish, including my parents, but I don't think that. They think everything's about qualifications and if you don't work hard in school, then no matter what else you're doing, you are not working hard.
>
> (Putwain, 2009)

It is important to clarify that although these concerns involve other people, they are not social anxieties of the type briefly outlined above. The person is concerned about how others might negatively judge academic competence, not social competence.

Also, failure can be threatening to one's future study or work aspirations. Particular grades in certain subjects, or a profile of subjects, may be required for entry into competitive university courses of professions. In some education systems and countries, all students have the opportunity to access higher secondary education. In England, Wales, and Northern Ireland, students take secondary school exit examinations (General Certificate of Secondary Education: GCSE) aged 15 to 16 years. In order to continue onto upper secondary education (called 6th form for anachronistic reasons) a student is often required to achieve a profile of pass grades or higher in GCSE examinations. Failure to achieve this profile of grades would mean following a vocational or technical alternative. Upper secondary education is the traditional route into university education and so failure in these exams (aged 15 or 16 years) may close off some educational opportunities and routes. A similar system operates in China where students sit the zhongkao (中考) examinations at the end of Grade 9 (aged 15 years) in order to access upper secondary education.

To summarise, test and exam anxiety results from the appraisal of a performance-evaluative situation as threatening. To this end, test and exam anxiety is often referred to as a *situation-specific* form of anxiety. Some highly test- and exam-anxious persons may become anxious in other specific (e.g., social), or even all, situations. However, this is not an important consideration solely for the assessment of test and exam anxiety. The important definitional issue here is that tests or exams are a specific type of situation that acts as a trigger for elevated anxiety in some people.

ARE TEST ANXIETY AND STRESS ANYTHING DIFFERENT?

When discussing the pressures associated with taking tests and exams, students, teachers, parents, and others, often use the words 'stress' and 'anxiety' interchangeably. That is, for some students, high-stakes exams are both a 'stressful' experience and an 'anxiety-provoking' experience. It is important to consider whether people are using these two terms to refer to the same experience of pressure or whether stress and anxiety might in fact be two distinct, but related, experiences. This is not a trivial question as stress and anxiety may be underpinned by different mechanisms, have different impacts on learning, information, processing, motivation, and exam performance, and therefore require dealing with in different ways.

My approach to disentangling the question of 'stress' and 'anxiety' has been to use the transactional model of stress and coping developed by Richard Lazarus and, in particular, a seminal study conducted with his colleague Elizabeth Folkman (Folkman & Lazarus, 1985). This theory of stress proposes that we differentiate between the demands made on someone, the perceived resources that someone has to respond to those demands, and the person's response to those demands. Demands refer to the pressures made of a person by a situation and are judged by their personal relevance to one's goals, aspirations, and well-being. In this theory, there are three basic types of demands: irrelevant, benign, and stressful. Demands are judged as irrelevant when they have no bearing whatsoever on one's goals or well-being, as benign when they will only lead to a positive outcome, and as stressful when they require some action on the part of the person where the outcome is uncertain. Demands are stressful when they could lead to gains on the one hand, but losses on the other.

The same situational demands, therefore, can be judged in different ways by the same person over time, and by different persons. If a person, for example, is asked to lead staff training on a new process, that task might be judged as irrelevant if that person does not care about the institution, colleagues, or the new process. This example is somewhat contrived as it would be unlikely that such a person would be asked to lead staff training, but it does serve to illustrate a point. If the person asked to lead to the training was highly skilled at leading staff training, was involved in the development of the new process, had evidence for proof-of-concept, and knew they were training a group of like-minded colleagues, perhaps that situation would be judged as benign. Everyone agrees the training will benefit colleagues and the institution. If the person leading the training was unsure that colleagues would respond favourably or they were not entirely confident of the value of the training, the situation could be perceived as stressful. That is, it could go either way. The training might be successful, and colleagues respond favourably, or it might not.

The demands made by tests and exams could be partly objective (e.g., I need a particular grade or profile of grades in order to be accepted into a university course, or a target grade provided by a student's school), and they could also be partly subjective. Subjective demands could be expectations made of oneself (e.g., meeting or exceeding a personal best, not wanting to let oneself down, and so on) and expectations we believe others have about us (family expectations, not wanting to let one's family down, and so on). If a student did not value schooling or qualifications (perhaps they have become completely disengaged and alienated from education) and there was no pressure from their family (perhaps family members also do not value schooling and qualifications and would prefer the student to join a family business), tests or exams would be judged as irrelevant. If a student strongly believed the test difficulty was low and they were very confident in their ability. it is possible they could judge the demands as benign, although this would seem unlikely with academic tests and exams as there is always an element that is out of one's control (e.g., the specific questions set, reliability of the marking, and so on).

Perhaps the most likely judgement of the demands is that they are stressful. That is, they require some action on the part of the person to meet those demands, such as exam preparation (e.g., learning the material to be examined and practising exemplar questions). According to the transactional model, a person can respond to stressful situational demands as a challenge or a threat depending on their perceived resources to respond. Resources can be environmental (e.g., access to the internet or a space to study), social (e.g., persons to provide academic advice or emotional support), and personal (e.g., confidence in one's ability or a belief that effort and persistence will pay off).

When resources are perceived to outstrip demands, the stressful situation is judged to be a challenge. When viewed as a challenge, the student believes that with effort they can meet the demand(s) posed by tests and exams and achieve their expected grade (whether a minimum pass or the highest grade possible). In a challenge state, the student is motivated, hopeful, engaged, and will make a good deal of effort in preparing for forthcoming tests and exams. Ultimately, their performance is better, and for these students, one might say that stress was a good thing.

When demands are perceived to outstrip resources, the stressful situation is judged to be a threat. When viewed as a threat, the student believes that they are unable to meet the demand(s) posed by tests and exams and they anticipate failure. In a threat state, the student can become anxious and worried, and their motivation may be directed towards reducing anxiety through distraction, avoidance, and procrastination rather than test and exam preparation. Paradoxically, this further increases the likelihood of failure. In extreme cases, students can withdraw effort as a means of self-worth protection. If one does not make any effort, there is a ready-made reason for failure that directs attention away from one's academic competence. For this student, stress was most definitely a bad thing and their learning and test/exam performance suffers.

When viewed from the perspective of the transactional model of stress and coping, stress and anxiety are not one and the same. Stress is neither a good nor bad thing in itself, and it depends on how the person responds to it. Put simply, stress can have good effects when appraised as a challenge and negative effects when appraised as a threat. Anxiety refers to a specific emotional reaction resulting from judging a stressful situation as a threat with typically negative consequences. One of the implications of this approach is that stress is not necessarily be something to worry about for students, parents, educators, and so on.

However, this point does come with a word of warning. In the long-term, stress is almost universally associated with negative outcomes such as emotional exhaustion and burnout. So, even if stress might be a short-term boost for engagement and test and exam performance, this response cannot be sustained in the long-term. Eventually, the person finds themselves in a permanent state of agitation, unable to sleep, developing a cynical attitude, and losing motivation.

The subtlety of many of these points is often missed in the academic literature and it is often not clear when claims are made about academic pressure or academic stress whether they are referring to short- or long-term stress, whether stress is referring to challenge or threat, or whether stress is being used as a proxy for anxiety. I would, therefore, encourage readers who may consult the academic literature, not to take findings at face value and check for how stress has been measured. It is only then that one will be able to understand whether the claims refer to short- or long-term stress, challenge or threat, or whether they really refer to anxiety.

WHAT ARE THE SIGNS AND INDICATORS OF TEST AND EXAM ANXIETY?

It is important that we have a clear understanding of the signs and indicators of test anxiety for both research and practical purposes. For research purposes, it is necessary to be able to measure test anxiety using instruments that can offer accuracy, precision, and consistency (the terms reliability and validity are used in the methodological literature). This can enable researchers to identify the antecedents, triggers, and causes of test anxiety, their outcomes and effects, and whether measures to support highly test-anxious students are effective. For practical purposes, instruments can be used to identify students for additional support, or intervention, and may be accompanied by typical ranges of scores at different ages and for different demographic groups (often called 'norms') and cut scores that indicate the score, or range of scores, that may identify different levels and type(s) or risk.

DIFFERENT COMPONENTS OF TEST ANXIETY

There is extensive evidence that test and exam anxiety comprises at least two distinct, but related, components. The first of these is a cognitive component, referring to worries about failure, and experiencing distraction and interference when learning, preparing for, and taking tests and exams. The second refers to the person's perception of the degree of physiological activation that occurs when anxious, both specific physiological reactions (e.g., a racing heart) and the more general 'feeling' of being tense and panicky.

This distinction has some important implications. These components may have different outcomes and respond to different types of intervention or support. Furthermore, while the physiological aspects of test and exam anxiety might be visible to an outsider, especially in extreme cases, the cognitive component is largely private and, therefore, relies on a person's self-report. Indeed, the assessment of test anxiety may only be possible at present through self-report. It may be the case in the future that accurate biophysiological indicators of test and exam anxiety can be identified from the balance between cardiac output and total peripheral arterial resistance, and endocrine responses but they are not available at the present time.

While there is a consensus that test and exam anxiety includes a cognitive dimension there is less agreement on whether worry should be defined narrowly or broadly. Narrow definitions of worry focus on the anticipation of failure and the negative consequences of failure. Broad definitions include, alongside these worries, concerns about one's performance or ability, preparedness for a forthcoming test or exam, comparing oneself to others, and worries about being judged negatively by others. My position is that this debate is best resolved by referring to theory and when we take this approach, concerns about being judged by others (and oneself) and one's competence or preparedness are reasons, or triggers, for why a person becomes anxious, not the anxiety itself. To avoid confounding the antecedents of anxiety with its indicators, it is better to adopt a narrow definition.

As we shall discuss in Chapter 5, one of the central reasons that persons become highly test-anxious is that their attention is dragged towards threat. There is an adaptive element to this process, as it can dedicate limited attentional resources towards dealing with, reducing, or perhaps even avoiding the threat. Consider a simple example: you are walking across the road and spot out of the corner of your eye an object travelling towards you quickly, like a speeding car you did not see when starting to cross the road. Detection of the threat allows you to take action to avoid being hit. Allocating cognitive resources to threat can be helpful not only when dealing with physical threats (like the above example) but also psychological threats. For instance, if a student responds to the threat of failure by expending effort in activities designed to minimise failure (e.g., revision, seeking advice from teachers, practice exam questions, and so on), this may indeed help to avoid failure (which as we have noted already may for some students be anything other than the highest grade).

This process can go awry, however, when the person cannot pull their attention away from the threat (e.g., thinking about failure and its consequences). Psychologists call the capacity we have to intentionally direct, or move, our attention from one thing to another (either in the environment or in the mind) attention control. When persons cannot direct their attention to planning and conducting revision, prior to an exam, or to thinking about how to answer a question during an exam, their learning and performance suffers. A common experience for highly test-anxious students is to experience 'going blank' in an exam and finding it difficult to recall from memory the material they have learnt in preparing for an exam. Another indicator of the cognitive dimension of test anxiety is, therefore, what psychologists call 'cognitive interference'.

The physiological element of test anxiety is the person's perception of the level of autonomic nervous system arousal. These comprise the perception of changes in specific organs. This may include, but is not limited to, a racing heart, churning stomach or feeling sick, becoming sweaty, and trembling hands and legs. Associated with the physiological component of test anxiety are the feelings produced by this autonomic nervous system activation, often referred to as the affective dimension. These include, but are not limited to, feelings of tension, dizziness, and panic. The key indicators of the cognitive, physiological, and affective components are listed in Box 1.1.

BOX 1.1 COGNITIVE AND AFFECTIVE-PHYSIOLOGICAL SIGNS OF TEST AND EXAM ANXIETY

Cognitive Signs of Exam Anxiety

- Going blank during an exam
- Difficulty concentrating
- Remembering answers after a test or exam has finished
- Worrying about failing a test or exam
- Worrying about past performance in tests or exams
- Worries about the consequences of failure

Affective and Physiological Signs of Exam Anxiety

- Feeling excessive tension
- Feeling panic
- Feeling dizzy or faint
- A racing or pounding heart
- Jelly/wobbly legs
- Shallow or short breaths

In addition to these cognitive and affective-physiological signs of test and exam anxiety, there are also behavioural and motivational aspects. On the one hand, these can include behaviours motivated by avoiding feelings of anxiety that we have already mentioned, such as, distracting oneself, procrastination, disengagement, and withdrawal of effort. However, on the other hand, they can also include behaviours underpinned by the motivation to avoid failure such as increased planning, effort, and persistence in exam preparation. Partly because of the divergence in behaviours motivated by anxiety (some positive and some negative), and partly because these study behaviours can be influenced by many things alongside anxiety, my position is that it is more straightforward to use the cognitive, and physiological-affective, signs of anxiety.

In addition to these general signs and symptoms of test and exam anxiety, there are standardised instruments available for use by practitioners and researchers. There are various instruments freely available to use each with its own advantages and disadvantages. With colleagues, I recently developed a new instrument based on a narrow definition of test and exam anxiety, which is the Multidimensional Test Anxiety Scale (MTAS; Putwain, von der Embse et al., 2021). Aligning with the different signs for test and exam anxiety outlined above, the MTAS contains two subscales each for the cognitive and affective-physiological components. The two cognitive subscales are for worry and cognitive interference, and the two affective-physiological subscales are for tension, and physiological indicators of anxiety. Researchers and practitioners can use either subscale or total scores depending on the intended purpose of measurement. Researchers may, for instance, wish to examine the measurement properties of the subscales, and their antecedents and outcomes of the different components. Practitioners may find greater utility in using a total score to identify students for additional support or intervention.

The benchmarks for developing and evaluating psychological tests, and also testing practices and the interpretation of results, are provided in a manual jointly produced by the American Educational Research Association, the American Psychological Association, and the National Council on Measurement in Education. The most recent manual (published in 2014) provides standards for the validity (i.e., that test scores can be interpreted accurately), reliability (i.e., consistency of test scores across different assessment points as well as the internal consistency of an instrument), fairness, and accessibility (i.e., barriers to the interpretation of scores for the widest possible of individuals and subgroups are minimised), and interpretation (i.e., norms and cut scores are available to support interpretation). The MTAS is the only instrument presently available that meets standards of validity, reliability, fairness and accessibility, and interpretation.

In particular, studies have demonstrated the validity of the four-component structure to measure either subscales or provide a total score and the internal consistency of subscale and total scores (Fenouillet et al., 2023; Putwain, von der Embse et al., 2021; von der Embse et al., 2021). Measurement properties have been shown to be equivalent for gender, age, and whether students are eligible for free school meals (a proxy for a low-income family background). Predictive validity has been shown for achievement, school-related well-being, and mental health risk. Finally, test-retest reliability has been shown meaning that, without intervention, MTAS scores do not vary much over time. Colleagues who may wish to use the MTAS can freely access the form and manual at: https://doi.org/10.17605/OSF.IO/T45YA.

CHAPTER SUMMARY

In this opening chapter, I have summarised research findings on how test anxiety is defined. From this body of work, we can understand that test anxiety arises from the perception that tests and exams present a broad psychological threat to one's self-worth. That is, failure will reflect negatively on one's academic competence and worthiness as a person. The more one values academic competence, or bases their self-worth on academic competence, the greater the perceived threat. We can also differentiate test and exam stress from test and exam anxiety. Stress can be a positive or negative thing arising from a challenge and threat response to pressure, respectively. Anxiety is a specific outcome arising from a threat response to pressure. Having defined test and exam anxiety, and differentiated it from stress, we rounded off the chapter by presenting its identifying characteristics and components, and how it can be measured.

A final point is that in some educational settings, the term 'test' implies a more informal, or non-standardised, form of assessment and 'examination' to a formalised, standardised assessment. With respect to test and exam anxiety this distinction is unimportant as they both represent a performance-evaluative situation. For this reason, in the remainder of this book, for brevity I will use the term exam anxiety as shorthand for test and exam anxiety.

2

HOW PREVALENT IS EXAM ANXIETY?

SETTING THE SCENE

What might seem a relatively straightforward question – that is, how many students experience severe exam anxiety – is fraught with difficulties. Few studies have considered this question, partly as there is no agreed criterion or standard for when exam anxiety becomes severe, and partly as it implies there is some kind of inherent categorical separation between those who are severely exam-anxious and those who are not.

An often-quoted statistic from a review paper of test anxiety published over 20 years ago (McDonald, 2001), suggested that between 10% and 41% of school-aged children were experiencing high levels of test anxiety. However, when we dig a little deeper, this statistic was derived from just three studies published between 1967 and 1994. One of these studies (Kondaš, 1967) identified students with 'stage-fright' rather than exam anxiety, and another was based on a sample of 59 elementary school children with an arbitrary cut-point for high test anxiety (Nottelmann & Hill, 1977). The third study (Turner et al., 1993), also of elementary school children, used a sample of 229 African American children and a cut-score for high exam anxiety based on likely risk for a clinical anxiety disorder established from previous research.

These three studies are not an adequate basis on which to make judgements about the current prevalence of severe exam anxiety. These studies were never intended to determine the prevalence of exam anxiety hence samples are small, one did not even measure exam anxiety, and they are all over 30 years old. The question of prevalence is one I have attempted to address in the last decade and in this chapter, I will describe some of the research I have conducted as well as that of others. In doing so, I will consider the various advantages and disadvantages of the approaches that were used to allow readers to inform their own judgements about the different approaches and what they might imply, and necessitates some description of methodological and analytic techniques.

WHAT ARE THE DIFFERENT WAYS IN WHICH HIGH EXAM ANXIETY COULD BE ESTABLISHED?

There are three possible approaches that could be used in isolation, or conjunction, to identify severe exam anxiety. These are (1) a norm-referenced approach, (2) a criterion-referenced approach, and (3) a statistical standard-setting approach.

THE NORM-REFERENCED APPROACH

In the norm-referenced approach, an arbitrary criterion (e.g., one standard deviation (SD) above the mean) is chosen based on the distribution of responses to an instrument like the Multidimensional Test Anxiety Scale (MTAS). Persons scoring at or above that criterion could be considered as 'severely' test anxious. We typically find that the distribution of test anxiety scores on an instrument like the MTAS follows what is called a normal (Gaussian) distribution, indicating that the majority of scores fall in the middle and there are fewer high or low scores. To illustrate the distribution of MTAS scores, I have plotted a histogram in Figure 2.1 based on responses from 1167 students in Years 7–13 from schools in England. The possible range of MTAS scores (16 through to 80) is shown on the x (horizontal) axis and the frequency (% of responses) with which those scores were chosen by students in the y (vertical) axis. Actual scores are shown in grey and an overlay of a perfect normal distribution is overlayed in black.

To be perfectly symmetrical, the mean (average), median (middle), and mode (most commonly occurring) scores would have the same value. This would result in 50% of scores above and 50% below, the mean, median, and mode. We can see from a visual inspection of Figure 2.1 that the distribution of actual scores is not a perfect (i.e., symmetrical) normal distribution but is close. The majority of MTAS scores fall in the middle of the scale range and there are fewer scores at closer to the lower end (nearer to 16) and the upper end (closer to 80) meaning that the distribution is not *skewed* towards lower or higher scores. In addition, the distribution of scores is not too pointy or flat (referred to as *kurtosis*).

If a sample of scores, like those in Figure 2.1 do not substantially deviate from that of a normal distribution, they can be used

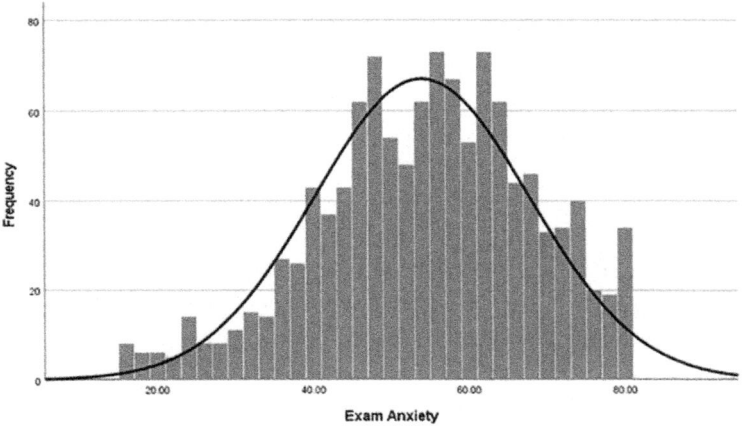

Figure 2.1 Histogram to Show the Distribution of MTAS Scores.

to identify the scores on an instrument for severely exam-anxious students. We can, however, be more precise than making a visual inspection of the distribution by considering the SD of the distribution of scores. An SD represents a section of the distribution around the mean. In a perfect normal distribution, 34.1% of the scores lie between the mean and one SD above the mean (+1SD), or 68.2% between one SD above and below the mean (±1SD). A further 13.6% of the scores lie between +1SD and +2SD, or 47.7% between the mean and +2SD, and 95.5% between ±2SD.

For the distribution of scores shown in Figure 2.1, the mean score was 53.99 and the SD was 13.88. The median and mode scores were both 55, 72% of scores fell ±1SD, and 95.9% of scores between ±2SD. These figures confirm what the visual inspection of the distribution shows; data were not precisely normally distributed (i.e., perfectly symmetrical) but were a close approximation. Hence, we can use data in this distribution to identify highly exam-anxious students. To establish what an MTAS score would be at +1SD, we can use the following formula:

$$\text{score} = \text{mean} + (\text{SD} \times z)$$

The z in the formula refers to a standardised unit of SD (where 0 is the mean and a single unit of SD is 1). To establish a MTAS score at +1SD, knowing the mean and SD of a sample, the calculation would be:

$$53.99 + (13.88 \times 1) = 67.87$$

A person with an MTAS score of 68 (if we round up 67.87) or more would then be considered to be severely test anxious. Often, instruments like the MTAS are accompanied by norms in the form of z-scores to assist interpretation. These show how many SDs a person's score would be above or below the mean of the statistical population that they were drawn from. Hence, if we wanted to know if a particular student was highly test anxious or not, we could ask them to complete the MTAS and compare their score to the MTAS norms. If a female student from England aged 15 years had an MTAS score 64, for example, we could consult the MTAS manual to find a z score of 0.9, meaning that (compared to others in the same statistical population) that person could be 0.9SDs above the mean. For a male student aged 15 years from England, a MTAS score of 64 would provide a z score of 1.36 (i.e., that person would be 1.36SDs above the mean).

The drawback of this approach is that a person is judged as severely exam-anxious or not relative to others. Whether a score of 64, for example, would be +1SD or not will depend on the mean and SD of the statistical population that they were drawn from. As female students report higher test anxiety scores on average than male students, a MTAS score of 64 would not be considered as severe for a female student (at +1SD) but would be for a male student. This makes it important that z scores are generated from a sufficiently large sample to be representative of the underlying statistical population. MTAS norms, for example, were derived from a sample of 6565 students, in England, aged 11–18 years (Putwain, von der Embse et al., 2021).

THE CRITERION-REFERENCED APPROACH

A criterion-referenced approach is one in which we set an absolute benchmark for what counts as severe exam anxiety. When a person reaches that benchmark, they would be considered as severely exam-anxious irrespective of the population mean. Benchmarks can be internal (i.e., derived from within the measurement instrument) or external (i.e., using something other than the measurement instrument). The response scales for Spielberger's (1980) Test Anxiety Inventory (TAI), a popular instrument for measuring exam anxiety, and the MTAS are shown in Figure 2.2. The TAI comprises 20 questions, and students respond on a four-point scale, providing a total score from 20 through to 80. The MTAS comprises 16 questions, and students respond on a five-point scale, providing a score

TAI Response Scale

Never	Sometimes	Often	Always
1	2	3	4

MTAS Response Scale

Strongly Disagree	Disagree	Neither	Agree	Strongly Agree
1	2	3	4	5

Figure 2.2 Response Scales for the TAI and the MTAS.

from 16 through to 80. We could take as an internal criterion on the TAI, for instance, persons who respond somewhere between 3 (often) and 4 (always) to all questions (e.g., "I feel very panicky when I take an important test"). This would mean a person scoring equal to above 60 out of 80 on the TAI (the 66th scale percentile) would be considered as severely exam-anxious.

Similarly, we could take as an internal criterion on the MTAS, persons who respond somewhere between 4 (agree) and 5 (strongly agree) to all questions (e.g., "During exams, I worry about the consequences of failing"). This would mean a person scoring equal to, or above, 64 out of 80 on the MTAS (the 80th scale percentile) would be considered as highly/ severely exam-anxious. Although these two examples result in different scale percentiles (66th for the TAI and 80th for the MTAS) either could be used. They are just applying different criteria to different response scales.

An external criterion would be establishing the point at which a certain level of exam anxiety could be harmful to one's typical or expected level of functioning. The educational risk could be, for example, achieving lower than a target, or predicted, performance. This approach would entail establishing if there was a score on an exam anxiety inventory (such as the MTAS) that could reliably predict one grade (for example) lower than would be expected for a particular student. This approach relies on the students' predicted grade that could be compared to a test or exam-generated measure of achievement. Target or predicted grades could be subject to their own biases depending on how they were generated.

In England, for example, the Department for Education uses a calculation from an organisation called the Fischer Family Trust (FFT) to generate a range of expected GCSE grades, at the end of secondary school-aged 16 years from National Curriculum test scores taken at the end of primary school (aged 11 years). If students were severely exam-anxious when they took National Curriculum tests aged 11, they may have been underperforming due to anxiety-induced interference. Therefore the range of FFT-derived predicted grades for GCSE exams may not be an appropriate method of judging relative education risk as they will also have been potentially biased by test anxiety. Of course, if students were not severely exam-anxious when taking National Curriculum tests then FFT predicted grades could be more feasible. There is no method of establishing predicted grades that is completely free from bias. Nonetheless, a combination of teacher assessments from class and homework combined with scores from low stakes tests (such as the cognitive ability tests many schools use) would result in a predicted grade that is less biased by test anxiety.

Mental health risk could, for instance, be judged against diagnosis of, or showing elevated symptoms of, a mental health disorder. This approach would entail identifying if there was a score on an exam anxiety inventory (such as the MTAS) which would reliably predict the likelihood of diagnosis with, for example, Generalised Anxiety Disorder (GAD), or the level at which symptoms of GAD are indicative of a likely diagnosis (see Table 4.1 in Chapter 4 for a brief description of these, and other, mental health disorders that could be linked to exam anxiety).

One advantage of this approach is that the cut-point for severe exam anxiety does not depend on the mean level reported by others. The disadvantage is that the threshold is somewhat arbitrary. For the internal criterion, there is no reason why one might choose an average response of 3 on the TAI (a total score of 60 out of 80) rather than 3.5 (a total score of 70 out of 80) in response to all questions. It purely depends on one's judgement as to where severe exam anxiety lies between *often* and *always*. In addition to the problem of bias discussed earlier in relation to the norm-referenced approach, the external criterion has the same issue. Would the educational risk be underachievement relative to a predicted or target grade? By one grade or two? One grade in all subjects or a single subject?

THE STATISTICAL STANDARD-SETTING APPROACH

A third approach is to establish, in a bottom-up data-driven fashion, whether there are relatively homogenous groups of responses of exam anxiety scores and if one, or more, such groups could represent a severe exam anxiety profile. This approach relies on statistical techniques called cluster analysis or latent profile analysis (LPA) (Sireci, 2001). The underlying idea is that if, for instance, we had 100 responses to an exam anxiety inventory, there would be, in principle, a maximum of 100 possible profiles. That is, a separate profile for each respondent. However, if several persons all showed the same scores (or thereabouts), it would be more economical to group those persons together into a cluster or profile. Statistical approaches do not provide a definitive number of profiles/clusters. Rather, one must make a judgement regarding the optimal number of profiles/clusters. This involves achieving a balance between clusters/profiles that are relatively homogenous, sufficiently distinct from others, and that account for a reasonable proportion of the sample. Similar to the norm-referenced approach, the number of profiles identified will depend on the characteristics of the sample, thus requiring a sufficiently large and representative sample. In addition, the eventual number of profiles is a matter of interpretation. Although this approach has not been specifically used to establish the proportion of severely exam-anxious students in England, I describe two examples of its use later in the chapter. One was to identify sub-groups of exam anxiety in US undergraduate students. The second was to identify groups of exam anxiety, alongside well-being, and symptoms of generalised anxiety and panic, in English and Welsh students aged 14–18 years.

A WORD OF WARNING REGARDING THE IDENTIFICATION OF SEVERELY EXAM-ANXIOUS STUDENTS

Each of the three approaches I have described has its own advantages and disadvantages. However, it is also important to highlight a more general issue arising from the identification of individuals or groups of severely exam-anxious persons. Anxiety is represented by an underlying distribution of scores, as presented in Figure 2.1, that is described as continuous. This means that, for the MTAS, a person could score anywhere from 16 (very low exam anxiety) to 80 (very high exam anxiety). The difference between MTAS scores is one of *degree*, that is, how much anxiety a person experiences around exams (sometimes described as a *quantitative* difference).

Establishing a cut-point from a continuous score is considered a controversial procedure by some as it implies there are two homogenous groups, those above and those below the threshold (DeCoster et al., 2009). For exam anxiety, persons identified with severe anxiety may need support, intervention, or exam accommodations, whereas those without, do not. Although this may sound plausible and practical, there is the danger that 'severe exam anxiety' is seen as categorical and shows a qualitative difference (i.e., one of *kind* not *degree*) with those who are not highly exam-anxious. In reality, if the cut-score for severe exam anxiety on the MTAS is set at 64, those with a score 63 (and hence *not* severely exam-anxious) will share more in common with those scoring 65 (and hence *are* severely exam-anxious) than a person scoring 25.

Nonetheless, cut-points can prove useful in practice as a simple and straightforward method to support decision-making. If it is known that severely exam-anxious persons underperform in exams due to anxiety-induced interference and they are at risk of poor mental health, then it is absolutely right to have an expedient method to assist their identification. In addition, schools and other agencies typically have limited resources at their disposal for additional support or intervention. Limited resources may need to be targeted at those most likely to benefit, and a cut-point for high exam anxiety may assist this process. The issues that are at debate here are referred to by psychologists and educational assessment specialists as consequential validity (Messick, 1995). That is, the positive and negative implications of how test scores are used. What is important is that we remain mindful that severe exam anxiety is not a difference of *kind* and that it is underpinned by a continuous distribution of scores.

In addition, the point at which a cut-score is established must be balanced against the consequences for students. The risk of identifying someone as severely exam-anxious when they are not (a false positive) may outweigh the risk of not doing so (a false negative). All things being equal, it may be better to offer additional support or intervention to a student who may only benefit slightly rather than withhold additional support or intervention from someone who may benefit greatly.

HOW MANY STUDENTS ARE IDENTIFIED AS SEVERELY EXAM-ANXIOUS?

In this section, I will present findings from research that has used the aforementioned approaches to establish how many students would be considered as highly/severely exam-anxious. With a colleague Tony Daly, I reviewed all of the UK-based studies using samples of secondary school-aged students up to 2013 and containing sufficient information with which to estimate severe exam anxiety (Putwain & Daly, 2014). Our literature review identified 10 studies from 2005 to 2011. Not all studies included information on the distribution of scores (i.e., the extent to which the distribution matched or deviated from a perfect Gaussian, distribution), ruling out a norm-referenced approach. Instead, we adopted an internal criterion-reference of the 66th scale percentile (i.e., if the study used a four-point response scale like the TAI, persons who responded *often* or *always* to every question). In the studies we reviewed, the proportion of the sample meeting this threshold ranged from 2.1% to 30.2%, with a mean of 15.1%. Many of the studies we identified, however, included only small samples as they were not intended to be used to establish the prevalence of severe exam anxiety.

To address the issue of sample size and representativeness, Tony and I collected new data from 2435 students (1,215 males, 1,220 females) in 11 secondary schools. Most students were in Years 10 (1218) and 11 (1121), with a smaller number from Year 9 (85). Importantly, this sample was representative of other students based in England for the proportions of students eligible for free school meals (a proxy for a low-income household), for whom English was an additional language, and achievement. Using the same internal criterion-reference (the 66th scale percentile; persons who responded *often* or *always* to every question), 16.4% of the sample were identified as highly/severely exam-anxious (female 22.5% and male 10.3%).

Using the large dataset of 6565 secondary school and 6th form students collected to demonstrate the validity, reliability, fairness and accessibility, and interpretation, of MTAS scores, I compared norm-referenced and internal criterion-referenced approaches to identifying severely exam-anxious students (Putwain, 2020). The threshold for the norm-referenced approach was +1SD and the results for male and female students at different ages is shown in Figure 2.3. In total, 12.3% of students were identified as highly/severely exam-anxious (female 16% and male 8.3%). Between the ages of 15 and 18 years when students were preparing for, and taking, high-stakes school exit exams, the total proportion was 14.1% (female 18.5% and male 9.8%).

The threshold for the internal criterion-reference was students who reported *agree* or *strongly agree* to all questions on the MTAS (80th scale percentile). The results for male and female students of different ages are shown in Figure 2.4. In total, 15.6% of students were identified as severely exam-anxious (female 18.8% and male 8.3%). Between the ages of 15 and 18 years, the total proportion was 16.9% (female 25.3% and male 8.5%). There are three notable

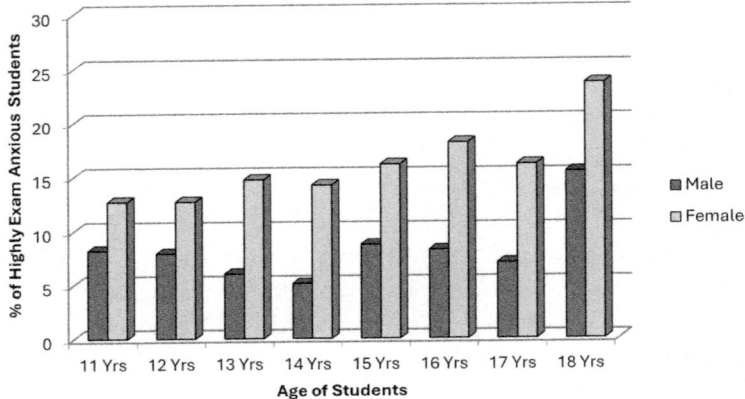

Figure 2.3 The Percentage of Students from English Secondary Schools Reporting High Levels of Norm-Based Exam Anxiety.

Note: Figure 2.3 was originally published in a British Academy provocation paper.

trends to highlight in these data. First, female students report higher levels of exam anxiety than male students. Second, exam anxiety is higher from age 15 years and upwards when students are preparing for and taking high-stakes exams. Third, in general, more students were identified as severely exam-anxious when taking the internal criterion-referenced approach than the norm-referenced approach.

In a second study of this type, Benjamin Lovett and colleagues (2024) collected data from 2,773 undergraduate students at a US University using the TAI. Using the 66th scale percentile (i.e., persons who responded *often* or *always* to every question), 29.8% of participants were identified as severely exam-anxious. By way of comparison, far fewer students (6% of males and 10% of females) were identified as severely exam-anxious if a norm-referenced approach was used (+1.5SD; 93rd scale percentile).

A study by Nathaniel von der Embse and colleagues (2021) is the only study, thus far, to have used an external criterion-reference. The external criterion was likely risk for a diagnosis of generalised anxiety disorder, characterised by excessive and persistent worry, and panic disorder (PD), current bursts of sudden severe anxiety and discomfort accompanied with dizziness, feelings of choking, and heart palpitations. In a sample of 918 participants (male = 217 and female = 694) from Years 10–13, drawn from eight secondary schools in England and Wales, a MTAS score of 58 (the 72nd scale percentile) was a reliable predictor of GAD diagnostic risk and a score of 60 (the 75th scale percentile) was a predictor of PD diagnostic risk. Taking the more conservative MTAS score of 60 would mean 35% of the sample would be judged as highly or severely exam-anxious. This is a higher figure than identified in the earlier studies (Putwain, 2020; Putwain & Daly, 2014) which may have been influenced by the greater proportion of female students in the sample; as we have seen in Figures 2.3 and 2.4, female students tend to report higher exam anxiety than male students.

A statistical standard-setting approach was used in a study of 807 (81% female with a mean age of 21.4 years) undergraduate students from the United States by Christopher Thomas and Colleagues (Thomas et al., 2018). This study used a 25-item instrument (Cognitive Test Anxiety Scale–Revised; Cassady & Johnson, 2002) with a four-point response scale of *not at all like me* to *very*

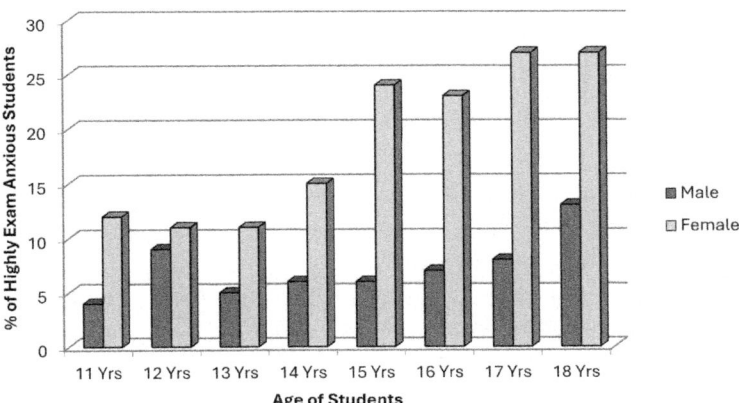

Figure 2.4 The Percentage of Students from English Secondary Schools Reporting High Levels of Internal Criterion-Based Exam Anxiety.

Note: Figure 2.4 was originally published in a British Academy provocation paper.

much like me (a total score of 25–100). Their LPA determined three profiles were optimal and comprised groups of high (22%), moderate (38%), and low (39%), exam anxiety. The cut-point for the high exam anxiety group was 67 (the 56th scale percentile).

What are we to make of the findings of these studies using different methods and based on different samples? First, the findings based on the studies I have conducted in England and Wales indicate that somewhere in the region of 15 to 17% of students aged 15–18 years are reporting high/severe exam anxiety. This percentage is higher for female students (up to 25%). A well-established finding that I will discuss in Chapter 3 is that severe exam anxiety is associated with lower achievement. We would expect, based on these findings, that many of the severely exam-anxious students may not be reaching their full potential and achieving less than they would do otherwise. No studies, however, have used an external criterion-reference of educational underachievement to establish a cut-score for educational risk. This would be an important piece of work that allows us to establish if it is possible to identify a point at which exam anxiety becomes sufficiently severe to reliably predict underachievement.

Studies have also linked severe exam anxiety to lower well-being and poor mental health. In addition, we have cut-points suggesting scores around the 72nd to 75th percentile indicate a risk of clinical anxiety disorder (GAD or PD). I would therefore conclude that ≈16% of severely or highly exam-anxious students are a real cause for concern and that their experiences should not be dismissed. We have a potentially large number of students aged 15–18 years who may be underachieving and exposed to pressures that are leading to dangerously high levels of anxiety.

Second, given that the relatively small number of studies that have considered the identification of cut-points, and that there is no agreed upon criteria for what constitutes severe exam anxiety, that we consider careful where to establish the criteria for severe exam anxiety. One must weight up, against the resources available for additional support or intervention, the consequences of potentially excluding those who would benefit by setting a cut-point too high.

A final point is to consider a finding from a study which was not principally concerned with identifying cut-points but does speak to the question of risk (Putwain, Stockinger, et al., 2021). This study considered exam anxiety alongside school-related well-being, and symptoms of GAD and PD and the same data-driven approach (LPA) as used by Thomas et al. (2018). The sample comprised students aged 14–18 years from England and Wales. A four-profile solution was optimal, and results are shown in Figure 2.5.

In Figure 2.5, the scale on the y (horizontal) axis is represented by z standardised scores. Although this sounds very technical, all it means is that a score of 0 would be the mean, a score of -1 would be 1SD below the mean, a score of +1SD above the mean and so on. The profile furthest on the left contained exam anxiety, GAD, and PD, scores that were all below the mean, and school-related well-being (SRWB) above the mean. This profile was labelled 'low risk' and was the largest group comprising 38.9% of the sample. The profile located immediately to the right contained exam anxiety, GAD, and PD, scores that were all above the mean, and SRWB below the mean. This profile was labelled 'moderate risk' comprising 21.5% of the sample. The next profile to the right contained the highest exam anxiety, GAD, and PD scores (all +1SD) and the lowest SRWB scores. This profile was labelled 'high risk' and, fortunately, was the

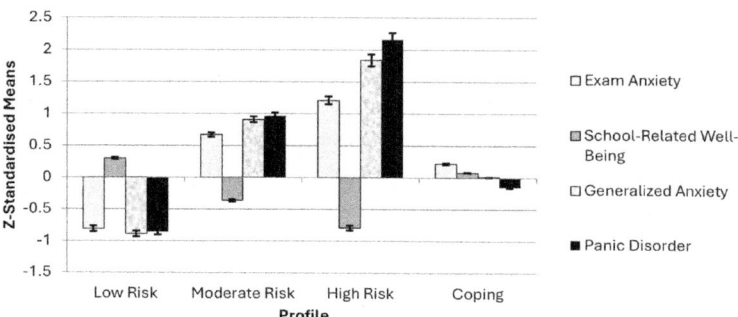

Figure 2.5 A Four-Profile Solution of Exam Anxiety, GAD, PD, and School-Related Well-being.

smallest group comprising 7.9% of the sample. The profile on the far right contained exam anxiety, GAD, PD, and SRWB, scores all around the mean. This profile was labelled 'coping' and comprised 31.7% of the sample.

These findings suggest that a relatively small group of students (7.9%) are presenting the highest risk, and these are the students most in need of support and intervention. This figure is notably smaller than the ≈16% of severely exam-anxious identified from the cut-score studies and suggests that at least some students may be resilient to their anxiety. Nonetheless, directly underneath the high-risk group were students with moderately high exam anxiety, GAD, and PD. These students may still require support or intervention but not as urgently perhaps as the high risk group or they may benefit from less intensive intervention. When resources are limited, a tiered approach could be implemented where the high risk group was offered targeted intensive intervention, whereas the moderate risk group could be offered less intensive intervention or workshops on effective coping with exam pressure.

A question I have been frequently asked in recent years is the extent to which reforms around the aforementioned high-stakes school exit exams by central government (introduced 2015–2018) have impacted exam anxiety. These reforms increased subject content and difficulty, moved to a norm-referenced grading system, and in most cases are assessed by terminal exams at the end of the course (rather than coursework or 'modular' exams taken throughout the course). This is not an easy question to answer due to the limitations of the data available. My interpretation of the data that we do have from English schools is that average levels of exam anxiety have increased slightly. For instance, Putwain and Daly (2014) identified 15.1% and 16.4% of secondary students as severely exam-anxious; Putwain (2020) identified 14.1% and 16.9% of students aged 15–18 years as severely exam-anxious; von der Embse et al. (2021)[1] identified 35% of students aged 13–19 years as severely exam-anxious.

In the last decade, however, there has also been a cultural shift. Children and young people, in the UK at least, have been encouraged to discuss issues affecting their mental health more openly than previously. I expect that many more adolescents taking high-stakes examinations are voicing their concerns to parents, teachers, and others, and this is resulting in a perception of an increase in exam anxiety (occurring during the same period that high-stakes exams were reformed) that is larger than the data suggests. This is partly due to a perception that the level of exam anxiety was *lower* than it actually was prior to exam reforms. The more relevant question for me, is why concerns around exam anxiety were *not* being taken with greater seriousness prior to the last decade in which exam reforms took place. They should have been.

Whichever identification approach is used (norm-referenced, criterion-referenced, or statistical standard-setting), the majority of adolescent students do not report severe exam anxiety. There are, however, still a significant number of students for whom severe exam anxiety could pose a risk of educational underachievement, poor mental health, and poor well-being (see Chapters 3 and 4). Many school and college leaders in England, and elsewhere, will know that the success or failure of an institution depends on how they deal with those students who are underachieving, or with poor attendance, behaviour, and so on. Attending to severely exam-anxious students is, therefore, a worthwhile effort for school and college leaders.

DEMOGRAPHIC DIFFERENCES IN EXAM ANXIETY

In this final section I shall consider findings from studies that highlight whether certain demographic groups report higher exam anxiety scores and, therefore, may be at greater risk of anxiety-induced educational underachievement and poor mental health. In the preceding section concerning the proportion of persons identified as severely exam-anxious, it was clear that in students of all ages, female students reported higher levels of exam anxiety. This is a finding that has been replicated in many studies of students of different ages throughout all regions of the world.

Meta-analyses, which combine and synthesise findings from individual studies, are extremely helpful in this respect. In one such meta-analysis, Nathaniel von der Embse and colleagues (2018) combined findings from 238 studies of students of all ages published from 1987 to 2017. This study, like many others, treated gender as a binary variable (man or woman). This does not discount the possibility of non-binary gender differences per se, but either there were insufficient numbers of non-binary genders to be included statistically as a separate category in the meta-analysis or that the primary studies on which the meta-analysis was based did not include categories of non-binary gender. Results showed that female students reported higher exam anxiety, but gender differences are small. Similar findings were reported in an earlier meta-analysis based on 562 studies of students of all ages from 1952 to 1986 (Hembree, 1988) and a more recent meta-analysis based on 76 studies of elementary and primary school-aged children (Robson et al., 2023).

While the evidence is quite clear that female students report higher exam anxiety than males, the interpretation of this finding is less clear. It is not clear the extent to which these findings represent 'real' differences or a bias in reporting. That is, something about the feminine gender role inclines persons to report higher test anxiety, and something about the masculine gender role inclines persons to report lower exam anxiety. Is it that female persons are accurate in their reporting and males are under-reporting, or vice versa? These are questions that we do not know the answer to.

However, they are part of a wider trend whereby female students' identity and social status, in general, are more closely tied to educational aspirations and they report higher levels of school-related stress (i.e., pressures that are unmanageable and threatening; Högberg & Horn, 2022). In addition, young females show higher general anxiety than males and higher rates of anxiety disorders, whereas young males tend to show higher levels of behaviours associated with externalising conditions such as aggression, rule breaking, poor impulse control (Chaplin & Aldao, 2013;

McLean & Anderson, 2009). My own view is formed partly from the research findings about school stress, anxiety disorders and externalising conditions and partly from working with adolescents experiencing severe exam anxiety for over 20 years; while there may be some element of gender-related bias in reporting exam anxiety, female persons do genuinely experience more anxiety than males.

Hembree's (1988) meta-analyses also showed that students from economically deprived backgrounds also report higher exam anxiety although, like gender, the difference is small. More recently, this has been shown to be the case for students in England using socioeconomic status (Putwain, 2007) and free school meals (von der Embse et al., 2021) as indicators of economic disadvantage. An analysis of the 2015 PISA data (389,215 secondary school students, aged 15 years, from 51 countries) showed not only that exam anxiety was higher in students from economically deprived backgrounds but also that the average exam anxiety from less affluent countries was much higher than from more affluent countries (King et al., 2023).

While these data show robust differences for economic deprivation and exam anxiety, like gender, the interpretation of the differences is not clear. It may be the case that the factors that lead persons from economically deprived backgrounds to typically show lower levels of achievement (e.g., less access to resources) also impact their exam anxiety either directly or indirectly as a function of a greater anticipation of failure. For societies with greater levels of income disparity, achievement may be a means of upward social and economic mobility placing more pressure on students.

Differences in levels of exam anxiety for students of different ethnic heritage have not been widely considered. In one of the relatively rare examples, Year 10 and 11 students who self-identified from Asian, black, or other,[2] backgrounds, in England, reported higher exam anxiety than students from White backgrounds (Putwain, 2007). Differences were small, however, and there were no differences between students for whom English was a first or additional language. However, this study only used crude categories of ethnic heritage when compared with the UKs Office for National Statistics approach that, for instance, contains five different categories of Asian or British Asian heritage (Bangladeshi, Chinese, Indian, Pakistani, or other), three categories of "black or British black heritage" (African, Caribbean, or other), give categories of white (Gypsy/Traveller, Roma, or other), and so on. There could also be differences within ethnic groupings that are as large (or even larger) than those between ethnic groupings.

Ethnic differences in exam anxiety are also included in the aforementioned meta-analyses. One of the difficulties of ethnic heritage data in meta-analyses is that the ethnic groups differ from one country to another. In the UK, for instance, the major ethnic groupings have been influenced by immigration from commonwealth countries and have typically included persons from Caribbean or South Asian countries. In the United States, major ethnic groupings include First Nation peoples (of Indigenous background), historical links to the slave trade (persons of African-Caribbean background), or proximity to central and south America (persons of Hispanic or Latino background), and persons of European background. In China, major ethnic groups include people from Han, Zhuang, and Hui, descent, as well as many others. In short, the makeup of ethnic heritage can look very different from one country to another. In addition, immigration contributes to a continuing evolution of the ethnic make-up of countries.

Perhaps one commonality across regions and countries is that persons from minority groups are subject to discrimination and receive less favourable treatment compared to the majority, and so this may represent one approach to combining studies from different countries. When classified this way, the meta-analyses have shown that persons from minority backgrounds report higher exam anxiety compared to the majority (Hembree, 1988; von der Embse et al., 2018). Davina Robson's approach was somewhat different and compared studies from differing world regions, finding that participants in studies originating from Asian regions reported higher exam anxiety than participants in studies originating from Europe and North

America (Robson et al., 2023). Whichever approach was used, however, the differences were small.

It is not possible to ascertain from this research whether the issue is one of discrimination or less favourable treatment resulting from belonging to a minority group characteristics of a particular ethnic grouping (e.g., greater parental pressure to succeed), or some combination of the two. Ethnicity is an area of research that clearly needs more work before we can draw solid conclusions. In addition, demographic characteristics intersect, resulting in complex combinations of gender, economic deprivation, and ethnic heritage. Differences in gender and economic deprivation, for example, may differ across ethnicity.

CHAPTER SUMMARY

In this chapter, I have set out the ways that it might be possible to identify severely anxious persons. Findings from different studies point to a figure of approximately 16%, which is higher (in studies mainly from England) from the ages of 15–18 years when students are preparing for and taking high-stakes school-exit exams (secondary school exit exams aged 16 years and upper secondary school exit exams aged 18 years). In addition, female persons and those from economically deprived backgrounds report higher levels of exam anxiety and so we would anticipate the proportion of high exam-anxious students from these groups would be higher.

NOTES

1   Also contained data from one Welsh school.
2   Other than Asian, black or white.

3

WHAT ARE THE CONSEQUENCES OF HIGH EXAM ANXIETY FOR EDUCATIONAL ACHIEVEMENT?

EXAM ANXIETY AND ACHIEVEMENT

The finding that exam anxiety negatively correlates with achievement of all types (including classroom-based assessment, teacher-estimated grades, exam performance, and so on) has been replicated in numerous studies. These negative correlations indicate that, all things being equal, persons who report higher levels of exam anxiety show lower achievement than persons reporting lower levels of exam anxiety. The meta-analyses (studies that combine findings from individual papers) mentioned in the previous chapter also provide insights into the nature of these correlations.

In Ray Hembree's (1988) meta-analysis (562 studies from 1952 to 1986), the average correlation in students from grade 4 upwards (i.e., students in elementary, secondary, and university education[1]) was −.29. In addition, there were no major differences across different subject areas, including reading and English, mathematics, social sciences, and natural sciences. Nathaniel von der Embse and colleagues' (2018) meta-analysis (238 studies from 1987 to 2017) broke down the correlations for students in different phases of education.

DOI: 10.4324/9781032716411-3

In primary education (grades 1–5) the average correlation was −.22, for intermediate education (grades 6–8) the average correlation was −.25, in secondary education (grades 9–12), the average correlation was −.16, and in post-secondary education (undergraduates and graduates), the average correlation was −.17.

In Davina Robson and colleagues' (2023) meta-analysis (76 studies of students in elementary and primary school from 2000 to 2020), the average correlation between exam anxiety and school achievement was −.23; studies looking specifically at mathematics showed an average correlation of −.21, literacy of −.20, and language at −.11. These meta-analyses, and others, combining findings from hundreds of studies and thousands of students (e.g., Robson's study included data from 13,169 individual students to estimate the average correlation between exam anxiety and mathematics achievement), point to a reliable finding. That is, higher exam anxiety is associated with lower achievement and appears to be consistent across age, or stage of education, and subject area (give or take some fluctuations). One caveat to this conclusion is that studies tend to focus on achievement in subjects traditionally assessed with written exams. It is not clear whether the same negative correlation with exam anxiety is found in subjects where assessments or exams with a greater emphasis on motor co-ordination (e.g., drama and music) or assessed on the production and narration of a creative artefact (e.g., art and design).

Readers might reasonably question the practical significance of these correlations. Correlations approaching ±1 are stronger and those approaching 0 are weaker. The range in the above-mentioned meta-analyses was −.11 to −.29; these are closer to 0 than ±1 and in classifications of the size of correlations would be considered as small. Small correlations, however, do not always imply a lack of consequence. As demonstrated in a study by Rosenthal and Rubin (1982), a correlation of +.2, widely considered to be small, equates to the success of an intervention improving from 40% to 60% (or conversely, −.2 would be the focus of a treatment declining from 60% to 40%). If the intervention in question was, for example, a treatment for stroke patients that improved rehabilitation, the correlation of

±.2 would not be considered as inconsequential. Why would it be any different for achievement?

In one study of 558 Year 11 students in England (the final year of secondary education), I examined the correlations between exam anxiety and exam performance in high-stakes school exit examinations (GCSEs) for English, mathematics, and science (Putwain, 2008). The correlation between the cognitive (worry) component of exam anxiety and aggregated grades in these three subjects was −.27; a 'small' correlation. This small correlation, however, was the equivalent of a two-grade difference in each of the three subjects between the highest and lowest exam-anxious students. I would not call the difference between a grade B (a pass) and a grade D (a fail)[2] in English, mathematics, and science, inconsequential.

We can also consider how exam anxiety fares against other so-called 'non-cognitive' or *soft* skills. A meta-analysis of 911 studies of university students between 1997 and 2010 (403,623 individual participants) by Richardson and colleagues (2012) included 42 non-cognitive skills, comprising different elements of personality, motivation, self-regulation, learning strategies, and social context. Exam anxiety showed the fifth strongest correlation with achievement (−.24) after performance self-efficacy (+.59; expectancy of success on a specific task), grade goal (+.35; a specific performance target), effort regulation (+.32; persistence with challenging work) and academic self-efficacy (+.31; general expectancy of success). The correlation between achievement and exam anxiety was also far stronger than that of achievement and socio-economic status (+.11) which is often the target of considerable policy focus and resources in the UK.

One further point to make is that correlations between exam anxiety and achievement are stronger for the cognitive component of exam anxiety (worry about one's performance and its consequences) than for an affective-physiological component (perceptions of tension and autonomic arousal); readers may wish to refer to Chapter 1 for an outline of these different components of exam anxiety. In von der Embse and colleagues' (2018) meta-analysis, the mean correlation with standardised exam performance was −.26 for the cognitive component and −.13 for the affective-physiological component. In Hembree's meta-analysis, the correlation with achievement was −.31 for the cognitive component and −.15 for the affective-physiological component. For comparative purposes, in the study I conducted, described above, the correlation between the affective-physiological component of exam anxiety and mean grade in aggregated grades for English, mathematics, and science was −.13 (Putwain, 2008).

The natural follow-on question is why there are differentially sized correlations for the cognitive and affective-physiological components of exam anxiety. The larger correlations observed for the cognitive component provide an indication of the mechanisms that explain why higher levels of anxiety may result in lower levels of achievement. In the next part of this chapter, I will turn to this issue and consider explanations of how exam anxiety may interfere with performance and perhaps also learning.

WHY DO HIGH EXAM-ANXIOUS STUDENTS SHOW LOWER ACHIEVEMENT?

One of the most prominent explanations of why exam anxiety (and indeed other forms of anxiety) negatively relates to performance is broadly referred to as cognitive interference. This idea is based on the principle that we have a limited range of cognitive capacity with which to perform any task. Psychologists often use the term 'working memory' to describe this cognitive capacity. Working memory does not just consist of memory, however; it includes other cognitive processes that we might use to complete a task. Such processes involve conscious and deliberate direction of one's attention and train of thought, switching back and forth between different tasks, recall from long-term memory, being able to temporarily keep two things in mind, and so on. The essence of interference theories is that anxiety, and worry specifically, interferes with working memory processes and capacity hence exam performance declines.

Readers who are teachers may be familiar with cognitive load theory. This theory, which has been gaining popularity in England following promotion by the school inspectorate, is like interference theories, based on the principle of a limited working memory capacity. The idea is that optimal learning should not overload working memory capacity. Instructional strategies to support working memory include breaking tasks down into component parts and using visual aids to represent task instructions and the steps required to complete an activity. When working memory capacity or processes are overloaded, task performance declines. The idea is similar to the way that worry occupies limited working memory resources. Complex tasks, which make greater demands of working memory capacity, increase the likelihood of overload. The automatisation of skills (including knowledge recall) through familiarity and repeated practice reduces the likelihood of overload. The increasing awareness of cognitive load theory in English educators has been largely confined to pedagogy. The same principles apply in exam settings too (as well as other performance situations).

For example, a recent question on the Pearson GCSE Mathematics Higher Tier Exam Paper from June 2022 (Pearson, 2022) was, "Work out $(4 \times 10^3) \times (6 \times 10^{-5})$. Give your answer in standard form". There are various approaches to answering this question, depending on how mathematics was taught, but it does require the candidate to complete several steps. For instance, one could begin by calculating 10 to the power of 3 (i.e., 10,000) and multiplying that figure by 4 (i.e., 40,000). One needs to hold the answer 40,000 in mind while then calculating 10 to the power of minus 5 (i.e., 0.0001). One must hold both the answer to the first operation (40,000) and the first part of the second operation (0.0001) in mind and multiply 0.0001 by 6 (0.0006). One can then arrive at the answer (24) by multiplying 40,000 by 0.0006. The question, however, requires the candidate to provide their answer in standard form (i.e., a number between 1 and 10). To transform 24 to a standard form, the answer would be 2.4×10^{-1}. Alternatively, one could multiply 4 by 6 (24) and $10^3 \times 10^{-5}$ (10^{-2}). We could then transform the result (24×10^{-2}) to standard form (2.4×10^{-1}). Of course, I am skipping over here the additional process required to transform a number to standard form.

Either approach would make a heavy demand on working memory resources if it was completed without the aid of a calculator (not allowed in this exam) or writing paper. One could easily forget the answer to the first part of the operation while mentally calculating one of the steps of the second operation. Persons well practised in mental calculation would find this task easier; automatisation has reduced demands on working memory. The use of pen and paper also reduces cognitive demand as one can write down the answers to the various stages rather than having to hold them simultaneously in memory.

Cognitive interference theories of anxiety have been around for half a century. One of the most recent and well-known theories is the Attentional Control Theory developed by Michael Eysenck and colleagues (2007). The central idea is that the focus of our attention is directed from two sources. One of these is top-down and refers to the intentional direction of attention to a particular task. This could be, for example, reading an exam question, thinking about how to answer the question, the steps involved in answering the question, and keeping focused on the question. The other source is bottom-up and refers to the perception of threat in our environment. If we detect a potential threat, our attention is directed towards that threat. It is assumed this threat-detection mechanism has evolved to perform a survival function. Indeed, we can see how such mechanisms are assistive in modern life when crossing busy roads or driving on motorways. Fast moving objects and loud, unexpected noises immediately capture our attention without any effort or intention on our part.

One of the downsides of this threat-detection mechanism, however, is that it also focuses attention on psychological threat. As I described in Chapter 1, the threat posed by exams is described as ego-threat; how failure may damage one's self-worth and aspirations or result in being judged negatively by others. Just as attention is directed to environmental threatwithout effort, attention is also directed to psychological threat without effort. This disrupts the very working memory processes that are needed to respond to the task demands. It is harder to recall information from long-term memory, it is more difficult to concentrate, it is harder to switch quickly between two or more tasks, and it is harder to hold two things in mind at the same time. Instead, the person's attention is self-focused on worries about their own competence, anticipating failure, and the negative consequences that might follow.

It is not difficult to see how the disruption caused to working memory processes will result in lower achievement. A common experience for many highly exam-anxious students during exams is to 'go blank'. That is, they simply cannot think, process information, or even if they have worked hard revising, recall relevant information from long-term memory. It can be instructive to consider how the experience is described by students themselves. The quotes in Box 3.1 are from interviews with students in Years 10 and 11 from England (Putwain, 2009):

BOX 3.1 QUOTES FROM STUDENTS IN YEARS 10 AND 11 TO ILLUSTRATE COGNITIVE INTERFERENCE

"…I remember it all before I get into the exam, but when I'm in the exam, my mind goes blank cos I'm nervous".

"I just read through the paper before I've filled in many of the things and it's like 'I just can't think' and I'll read the same question over and over again and I just can't get it to go in my head. I just keep reading it and it's just not going in and I'll make stupid mistakes like things that are really obvious like reading the question properly".

"…when you walk out of the exam and relax it all comes flooding back, all the stuff".

The short extract in Box 3.2 is from an interview I conducted with an English Year 11 student. It has not been published but is included in the training for an exam anxiety intervention used by the British Psychological Society.

BOX 3.2 EXTRACT FROM AN INTERVIEW WITH A YEAR 11 STUDENT TO ILLUSTRATE COGNITIVE INTERFERENCE

INTERVIEWER: What would you say makes you anxious?

STUDENT: I really struggle in maths. If I can't quite figure out a certain topic, I just go into panic mode and it's almost like a brick wall comes down in front of me and I just don't know what to do.

INTERVIEWER: Is this when you're in a test or in one of your assessments?

STUDENT: Yes [in a test or controlled assessment], or even just in class. If I don't understand it, I'll just stop and I find I can't do anything.

INTERVIEWER: OK, in class as well. So, when you say you panic, what's happening in that moment?

STUDENT: It's like I freeze. I just don't know what to do about it. I just sit there and stare at the paper.

The quotes and interview extract illustrate how anxiety interferes with cognitive processes. It is not difficult to imagine how distressing and frustrating this must be for the individuals concerned. They could expend an extraordinary amount of effort preparing for exams and yet not have the opportunity to demonstrate their learning and knowledge. Exams with greater cognitive demands will result in greater working memory disruption and a greater familiarity with exam questions and their recall (i.e., automatisation) will help to reduce cognitive demands and the subsequent working memory disruption. Exam questions that require rigid ways of thinking and/or fact-based recall may benefit more from automatisation as answers can be rote learned.

Research supports this claim. In a meta-analysis of 177 studies (with 22,061 individual participants), Tim Moran (2016) showed anxiety was negatively, and consistently, correlated with working memory performance. A series of studies by Matthew Owens has also shown how the negative correlation between anxiety and achievement is not direct. Rather, as predicted by Attentional Control Theory, the relation is indirect. That is, higher anxiety predicts impaired working memory function and, in turn, impaired working memory function predicts lower achievement. In methodological parlance we would say that working memory function *mediates* (i.e., explains) the negative relation between anxiety and achievement.

In one study of children aged 11–12 years, working memory function was shown to mediate the negative correlation between anxiety and performance in Year 6 National Curriculum Tests for numeracy and literacy and the quantitative, verbal, and non-verbal reasoning scores in the CAT3 Cognitive Abilities Test (Owens et al., 2008).[3] A notable limitation of Moran's meta-analysis, and Owens' studies of mediation, is that they relied on general measurements of anxiety rather than exam anxiety specifically. We would expect the precision offered by measuring exam anxiety specifically to result in stronger correlations. Nonetheless, they do provide a foundation for the role of working memory in the relation between exam anxiety and performance.

Attentional Control Theory also proposes that the detection of threat motivates the person to take action to reduce or avoid the threat. Thus, the highly exam-anxious person may make a compensatory effort in exam preparation and, during the exam, expend greater mental effort in purposefully moving effort from self-focused worries to answering exam questions. That is easier said than done as the threat-detection system keeps returning attention to the source of the threat. I conducted one of the few studies to test this idea with Wendy Symes (Putwain & Symes, 2018). We measured the exam anxiety and effort in school-work and exam preparation in secondary school students preparing for their high-stakes GCSE school exit examinations. Results (as shown in Figure 3.1) showed a negative correlation between exam anxiety and aggregated grades in English, mathematics, and science. Exams were graded on an eight-point letter scale, meaning a score of 24 would be the highest possible grade (A★) in these three subjects and a score of 3 the lowest possible grades (G). A score of 15 would indicate an average pass grade (C) in all three subjects. The negative correlation was stronger in students reporting lower effort and weaker in students reporting greater effort (i.e., high effort reduced the negative impact of exam anxiety on exam performance).

It is notable that even with average levels of effort, the relation between exam anxiety and performance is negative (i.e., greater anxiety is associated with lower achievement) for the typical student. It may be the case that the impact of working memory impairment outweighs compensatory effort. However, it is also the case that some highly exam-anxious persons may focus more on avoiding feelings of anxiety through distraction, mentally disengaging in lessons, procrastinating exam preparation, and so on. While these

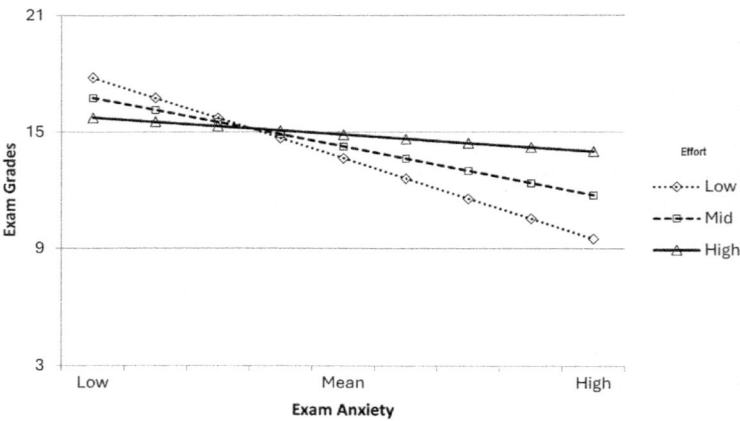

Figure 3.1 High Effort Reduces the Negative Impact of Exam Anxiety on Exam Performance.

strategies may have a short-term beneficial effect (i.e., reducing negative feelings) they are not good long-term strategies. The student can easily become trapped in a vicious cycle of exam anxiety triggering avoidance, which subsequently increases the likelihood of failure, and maintains the exam anxiety, more avoidance, and so on. This is an idea we shall explore in greater detail in Chapter 5. Put simply, students may know that exam preparation is the best way to maximise their chances of success and reduce the threat of failure. However, for some students the distress triggered when thinking about exam preparation, let alone starting it, is severe enough to present a serious obstacle in doing so.

Attentional Control Theory and other cognitive interference explanations propose a causal role for exam anxiety. That is, exam anxiety is the *cause* of lower achievement (via working memory impairment). One of the limitations of the evidence from *naturalistic* studies, making use of samples of students from schools, colleges, and universities, and their achievement, is that it can be difficult to show causality. As we have described above, exam anxiety negatively correlates with achievement, but does not mean the anxiety is the *cause* of low achievement. It could be the opposite that low achievement is causing the anxiety. The only way to show conclusively that anxiety is the cause of low achievement is to conduct an experimental study (sometimes called a randomised control trial) whereby we induce a high level of anxiety in some students to observe its effect on achievement. Such a study would not be ethical in a real-life setting; we could potentially interfere with a person's life chances purely to resolve a theoretical argument. Of course, such studies may be permissible, with a limited degree of anxiety induced in a lab setting where the consequences were not so impactful. However, a question will also remain over the transferability of the findings from the lab to the real-life setting.

In naturalistic studies, trait exam anxiety is often measured weeks or months in advance of the exams to avoid interfering with exam preparation. The time lag from measuring exam anxiety and exam performance is advantageous in naturalistic designs. If variable

x (i.e., exam anxiety) is the cause of variable y (i.e., low achievement) then x must occur before y. Low achievement occurring *after* the measurement of exam anxiety cannot be the cause of that anxiety. To be the cause of high anxiety, low achievement would have to be measured *before* exam anxiety.

It could be the case, however, that prior low achievement was causing students to anticipate failure and hence become anxious. In addition, low prior achievement could *also* be the cause of subsequent low achievement. In this case the positive correlation between exam anxiety and subsequent low achievement is just an artefact of prior low achievement. Anxiety is not driving low achievement. The implication for naturalistic studies is that correlating exam anxiety at one point in time with exam performance at a later point in time is not enough. We also need, at a minimum, to include prior achievement. In methodological parlance we would say to *statistically control* for the influence of prior achievement.

If negative correlations between exam anxiety and subsequent achievement become negligible once prior achievement, or cognitive ability, is statistically controlled for, this would point to prior low achievement driving both higher exam anxiety and lower subsequent achievement. If, however, the negative correlation between exam anxiety remains when prior achievement is statistically controlled for then higher exam anxiety remains a driver of lower achievement.

In one such study I conducted with colleagues (Putwain et al., 2013), students in the final year of primary school (Year 6) completed Raven's Progressive Matrices near the beginning of the school year in September. Raven's Progressive Matrices provide a measure of non-verbal ability by presenting a series of geometric shapes with one missing. The student completing the matrices must select the missing shape from a range of options. Later achievement was taken from National Curriculum Tests in literacy, numeracy, and science, taken the following May. Exam anxiety was measured two weeks before the tests. As expected, Raven's Progressive Matrices scores correlated strongly with scores on the National Curriculum Tests.

Importantly, exam anxiety was still a negative predictor of National Curriculum Test scores, after the relation with ability (measured from the Raven's Progressive Matrices) was statistically controlled for.

In a second study (Putwain et al., 2016), myself and colleagues showed that exam anxiety remained a negative predictor of GCSE achievement in English, science, and maths when statistically controlling for National Curriculum Test scores taken five years earlier. Both of these studies show that exam anxiety *drives* subsequent low achievement. It is not the same as saying it *causes* low achievement. It does rule out, however, the possibility that anxiety and subsequent achievement are both an artefact of prior low achievement or cognitive ability. What is ideally needed is a study with multiple points of measurement over a period of time so that we can test whether lower achievement also drives higher anxiety (having statistically controlled for prior anxiety) as well as higher anxiety driving subsequent lower achievement. This type of study would examine whether anxiety and achievement are *reciprocally related*. Studies have shown reciprocal relations between learning-related anxiety and achievement (Litchenfeld et al., 2022; Pekrun et al., 2017; Putwain et al., 2021). While learning-related anxiety is similar to that of exam anxiety, it is not identical, and studies are needed to examine reciprocal relations between exam anxiety specifically.

CAN A "BIT OF STRESS" BE A GOOD THING FOR ACHIEVEMENT AND EXAM PERFORMANCE?

When discussing how exam anxiety relates to achievement, I am often asked the question "can a bit of stress be a good thing?" The idea is partly underpinned by people's direct experience (or what they have witnessed in others) that performance has improved when they felt under pressure. Sometimes I hear comments like "I needed a bit of stress to get me going". The idea is also partly grounded by a widely held assumption that the relation between arousal of the autonomic nervous system and performance follows an inverted U-shaped pattern. This is often referred to as the Yerkes-Dodson

Law (see Figure 3.2). Consider, for example,, how this relationship compares to those shown in Figure 3.1. In Figure 3.1, the lines are straight rather than curvy. In statistical terms, we refer to these straight-line relations as *linear*. The linear relation between exam anxiety and achievement would propose that low anxiety does not harm achievement. As anxiety increases, the detriment to achievement shows a corresponding increase. In contrast, the Yerkes-Dodson Law proposes that moderate anxiety is actually beneficial for achievement. It is only once anxiety passes beyond a moderate level that it becomes detrimental. In statistical terms, this type of inverted U-shape relation is referred to as a *curvilinear* relation or to be more precise, a *quadratic* relation (as there are different types of curvilinear relations).

The idea behind the Yerkes–Dodson Law is problematic for numerous reasons. First, the terms stress, anxiety, and arousal, are used as if they mean the same thing. I attempted to unpick some of the differences between anxiety and stress in Chapter 1. Short-term stress can result in positive (challenge) and negative (threat) states both of which involve physiological arousal. Anxiety, however, is a specific response to threat. It has not helped when different versions of this inverted U-shape relation are presented in textbooks

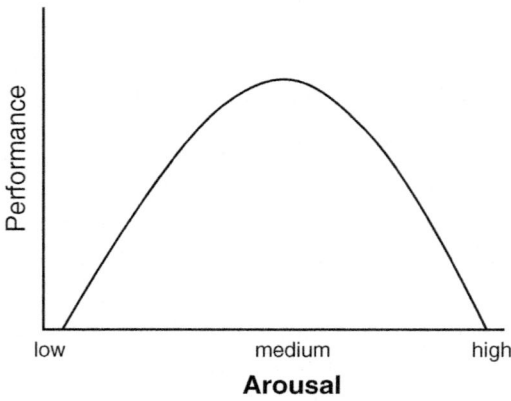

Figure 3.2 The Inverted Relation Between Arousal and Performance.

with the labels arousal, stress, and anxiety, used on the x (horizontal) axis interchangeably. The use of different labels implies stress, anxiety and arousal are similar.

Second, the Yerkes-Dodson law is, perhaps not unreasonably, associated with a study in 1908 by Robert Yerkes and John Dodson. Readers may be surprised to hear that their study contained no reference to a 'law', was not about arousal (or stress or anxiety), and was not even about humans! In fact, it was a study of how mice responded to mild painful stimuli in learning. The "Yerkes-Dodson Law" actually originates from the 1950s when it started to be used by psychologists considering how human motivation related to performance (Broadhurst, 1959). They often drew, like many psychologists of the time, from research based on animals hence the link to the 1908 study by Yerkes and Dodson.

Subsequently, the Yerkes-Dodson Law seems to have taken on a mythical status. It appears in numerous introductory psychology textbooks (and websites) as if fact. The third problem, and the biggest in my view, is the lack of evidence for it. Remarkably, few studies have tested whether the relation between exam anxiety and achievement is curvilinear (quadratic or otherwise), and of those that have, not all have used appropriate measures of exam anxiety. For example, a study of Taiwanese secondary school students with a mean age of 15 years claimed to have found an inverted U-shaped relation between exam anxiety and exam performance (Sung et al., 2016; see Figure 3.3). However, exam anxiety was measured using a scale that combined included social concerns (e.g., jealousy of other students) and study behaviours (e.g., working hard) alongside physiological anxiety responses, making it difficult to draw conclusions.

More recently, Ronnel King and colleagues (2024) examined data from the 2015 Programme for International Student Assessment (PISA) study. This is a large dataset comprising 389,215 secondary school students aged 15 years, from 51 countries. Results for the relations between exam anxiety and tests for reading, maths, and science are shown in Figure 3.4. Test score is represented on the y (vertical) axis and exam anxiety on the x (horizontal) axis. In the reading and

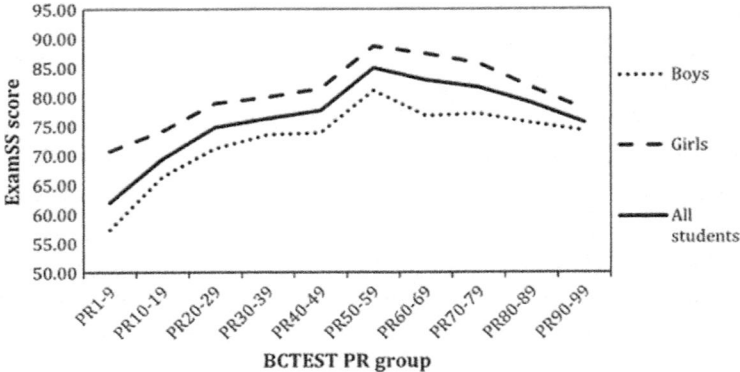

Figure 3.3 The Curvilinear Relation Between Exam Anxiety and Achievement (Sung et al., 2016, p. 248).

Note: Exam anxiety is represented on the y (vertical) axis as examination stress scale (ExamSS) scores and test performance on the x (horizontal) axis as Basic Competence (BC) Test scores. These are divided into percentiles. PR1-9 is the bottom 1–9% of scores, PR10-19, the next 10% of scores, and so on.

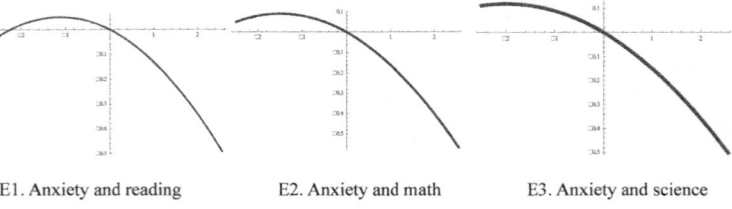

E1. Anxiety and reading   E2. Anxiety and math   E3. Anxiety and science

Figure 3.4 The Curvilinear Relation Between Exam Anxiety and Achievement (King et al., 2024, Supplementary Materials, p. 2).

maths tests, the facilitating impact of low to moderate anxiety was slight and nothing as impactful as suggested in the Yerkes Dodson Law. From moderate anxiety onwards, the relation was negative and largely linear. The facilitating impact of low to moderate anxiety for science is virtually absent. Other studies have also pointed to the facilitating impact of low to moderate anxiety being very small (Keeley et al., 2008) or entirely non-existent (Cassady et al., 2024; Schillinger et al., 2021).

Building on this idea, the fourth problem is that the Yerkes–Dodson Law does not consider the differences between challenge and threat states. To briefly remind readers, challenge is where a person believes that they have the resources (situational or personal) to meet the demands made on them by the situation. Threat is where the person believes the demands made by their situation outstrip their resources. Both challenge and threat come under the banner of stress and both involve activation of the autonomic nervous system (e.g., elevated heart rate, sweaty palms, stomach discomfort, and shallow breathing).

However, there are other physiological indicators that differentiate challenge and threat (Seery, 2011). In a challenge state, the heart beats faster, and arteries dilate due to the release of adrenaline. This allows the blood to move around the body effectively without an increase in blood pressure, similar to what happens during aerobic exercise in a healthy person. In a threat state, a faster heart rate is coupled with the release of cortisol which inhibits arterial dilation resulting in increased blood pressure.

Psychologically, people feel motivated and energised in a challenge state. They believe that success is possible, work harder than they usually do, and as a consequence can perform better than they could have done otherwise. When people say "a bit of stress can be a good thing", a challenge state is what they are referring to. The hypothetical relation between stress and performance for challenge and threat states is plotted in Figure 3.5. For a challenge appraisal, as the level of stress increases, performance shows a corresponding increase. After a certain point, however, the benefits afforded by a challenge state tail off.

In threat state, people feel overwhelmed, anticipate failure, and become worried and anxious. They are low in confidence, do not believe in themselves, and either do not know where or how to seek educational support, or are too uncomfortable to ask. For a threat appraisal, as stress increases, performance decreases. This expected pattern of results is similar to that shown between anxiety and performance in Figure 3.4. In practice, zero anxiety may indicate complete task disengagement hence there is a very small facilitating effect, although nothing as strong as suggested in the Yerkes Dodson Law. Anything other than a very small amount of anxiety is damaging to achievement.

The relation between a threat state and performance has been evidenced many times through the negative correlation between exam anxiety and achievement, even if the majority of studies model that relation as linear rather than accounting for the curves seen in Figures 3.4 and 3.5. Studies comparing challenge and threat states are more limited. In one study, Justin Travis and colleagues (2020) compared challenge and threat stress states for a sample of

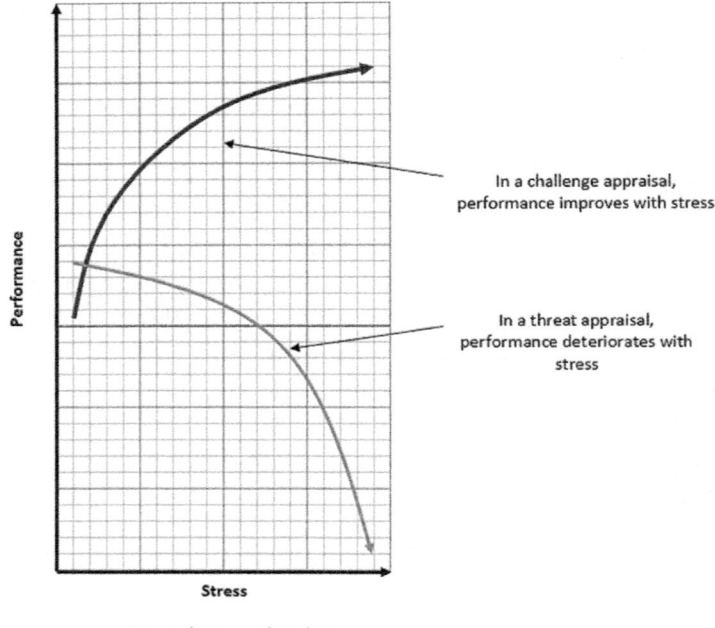

Figure 3.5 The Hypothetical Relation Between Stress and Performance for Challenge and Threat States.

American undergraduate students. Students' overall achievement was higher, and drop-out was lower for students who interpreted stress as a challenge. The opposite pattern was shown for a threat state; achievement was lower, and drop-out was higher.

Closer to home, I have conducted a series of studies looking at how students respond to messages from their teachers about the importance of performing well in high-stakes exams such as GCSEs (e.g., that grades in particular subjects, like English and maths, are essential for continuing in education or getting a good job). Students' experience of those messages depends on whether they respond to them as a challenge or a threat. When experienced as a challenge, messages are appraised as motivating, students are more engaged in their work and perform better (Putwain et al., 2021). When experienced as a threat, messages are perceived as pressuring, students are less engaged in their work, and perform worse (Putwain et al., 2021).

I am amazed the despite all of the evidence to the contrary, a belief in the Yerkes-Dodson law persists. To my mind, it is a dangerous myth. As I hope that I have explained in this chapter, it is not the *amount* of stress that determines whether performance is helped or hindered, but the *type*; that is, whether the stress refers to a challenge or threat state. One of the most important messages we can communicate to students of all ages preparing for, and taking, high-stakes exams, is that stress is nothing to be scared about. Stress can be beneficial for achievement (in the short-term) and we can learn to respond to stress positively as a challenge rather than as a threat. This idea is something that we will revisit in Chapter 6.

RESPONDING TO STRESS AS A CHALLENGE RATHER THAN A THREAT

All things being equal, a challenge response enables greater motivation, engagement, persistence, and performance, whereas threat hinders motivation, engagement, persistence, and performance. One recommendation would be, therefore, to help students respond to pressures as a challenge rather than a threat. Although I am usually quite suspicious of these kinds of recommendations as being too utopian (or perhaps even dystopian) in their ideals, there is a grain of truth within them. The following six recommendations present some general principles that can be incorporated into pedagogy and used to create a classroom atmosphere that is conducive to a challenge, rather than threat, response. They are drawn from the work I have conducted on challenge and threat responses to the language used around GCSEs, as well as work others have conducted on motivation (Eccles & Wigfield, 2020) and growth mindset (Yeager & Dweck, 2020).

The general idea is that students' value of a particular subject area, achievement, and education more generally, combine with the expectation of success to drive aspiration and achievement. Value provides the reason for making an effort in one's school-work (*why do I want to do this?*) and expectancy, underpinned by competence beliefs such as academic self-concept and self-efficacy, the belief that one is capable (*can I do this?*). Cost, what is lost or given up, hinders aspiration and achievement (is this *too much* effort; should I make an effort in *something else*?).

First, teachers can raise aspirations and achievement through showing enthusiasm for their subject and for teaching their subject, and by communicating to students the usefulness and importance of their subject through drawing links between the curriculum and how that understanding is used in multiple areas of life (referred to as utility value). Showing enthusiasm and communicating value raises students' own values and reduces their costs, which subsequently positively impacts aspirations and achievement. Demonstrating authentic enthusiasm and discussing the contribution of science to everyday life with students are 'easy wins' for teachers and schools.

Second, intrinsic value in a subject can be raised through lessons and activities designed to stimulate curiosity and interest. Raising the value of attainment is a double-edged sword. Attainment value is primarily raised through students' internalising the link between achievement and self-worth, or self-esteem. Raising attainment value can drive students to greater aspiration and achievement but can also flip into a fear of failure and backfire; it is a high-risk strategy and given the relatively low costs of raising intrinsic and utility value, these would be better values to focus on.

Third, school leaders may wish to consider additional strategies to raise (accurate) expectations. Expectations of success do not necessarily map logically one-to-one with ability. This is because students judge their competence in a subject from numerous sources, including (a) the perceived difficulty of classwork and homework, (b) feedback on classwork, homework, and other forms of assessment such as tests and exams, (c) comparing themselves with peers, classmates, and family members, and (d), comparing the perceived difficulty of work and feedback from one subject to another. Hence, a student in a top set who perceives themselves to struggle in comparison to their classmates may actually have a lower expectation of success than a student in a lower set who perceives themselves to be academically superior to their classmates. It is impossible to prevent students judging their competence to others in classroom settings; however, student expectations can be strengthened through:

a. providing feedback to students that enables them to understand the reasons why they demonstrated a correct understanding or not, or the strengths and weaknesses in their work
b. providing strategy-focused feedback on work; that is, to show students concrete actions they can take to improve their understanding or performance
c. avoiding feedback that praises a student's ability or encourages comparison with other students or other subjects
d. designing lessons and activities with an optimal challenge level for students; that is, work is challenging, but not too difficult.

Fourth, many of these aforementioned points will also focus on reducing perceptions of cost. In addition, strategies designed to reinforce the importance of effort (especially combined with strategy-focused feedback; based on the principles of 'growth mindset') will help to offset costs. Strategies designed to break the link between making mistakes and failing (fostering the belief that making mistakes are part of learning; especially when combined with strategy-focused feedback) will help to offset cost.

We can liken these suggestions as helping students to build a student's toolbox of personal resources that they can draw on to deal with the demands posed by preparing for, and taking, tests and exams. They will only be effective, however, if students are confident if they know how to plan to study for an exam, which study strategies to use (and these may differ from one subject to another), and whether their study has been effective or not. Many schools and colleges will already be incorporating goal setting, study planning, and study skills, into their exam preparation activities with students. I would recommend that students are shown how to judge the effectiveness of their exam study in a low-stakes setting and then to reflect on whether their study goals have been met or to inform the setting on new goals.

In addition to these principles that can be incorporated into a motivationally enhancing pedagogy and classroom environment, I would recommend discussing the issue with stress with students in an assembly or other group forum. The idea is to present to students some basic ideas about stress, how it arises, that stress is to be expected under pressured circumstances and that stress is not something to be scared of. The following slides and text are suggestions for issues and idea that could be incorporated into an assembly on exam stress (Figures 3.6–3.12).

These are just some initial suggestions. Colleagues working in schools and colleges may wish to add to these with slides showing to students how they help to ensure they respond to exam pressures as a challenge through using effective revision strategies, identifying and challenging thoughts that put additional (and sometimes unnecessary) pressure on oneself, and using relaxation strategies (like diaphragmatic breathing), to overcome panic. These are all ideas that I will expand on in Chapter 6.

> STRESS IS NOT NECESSARILY A BAD THING!

Figure 3.6 Some people are under the misapprehension that stress is a harmful or damaging thing. The first point to make is that stress is *not necessarily* a bad thing. For some people, stress is a great motivator that drives them to achieve things that they wouldnot have achieved without that stress, whereas for other people, stress becomes negative and causes people to 'choke' under pressure. Different people react to stress in different ways. To understand why people react to stress differently it is necessary to understand a little about how stress arises.

> Stress comes from a combination of:
>
> (1) The **demands** that are placed on you
>
> (2) The **resources** you have (or **believe** you have) to respond to those demands

Figure 3.7 This slide presents the two basic factors that determine whether stress is experienced as a good thing or not. Stress arises from the combination of the *demands* that are made of us (our time, energy, expertise, emotion, and so on) and *resources* that we have to respond to those demands. Resources can be actual (e.g., supportive and helpful peers, parents, teachers, and so on) and perceived (e.g., confidence in one's ability, a strong belief in effort, and so on).

Demands

- Pressure you put on your **self**
  "Unless I get my target grades, I'll feel like a failure"

- Pressure from your **family**
  "I'm always being compared to my cousin"

- Pressure from **school**
  "I'm always being told how important my exams are to get a good job or get into college"

Figure 3.8 This slide presents an example of a demand relevant to exam stress. High-stakes make many demands of students, so it is entirely normal to experience them as stressful. One example of a pressure might be the expectations that a student has to achieve their target or expected grades. They could think to themselves, "I must achieve these grades, if I do not I am a failure". Such internally generated thoughts add to the pressure that a student experiences. Other pressures can come from parents, peers, siblings, and other family members (intentionally or otherwise). Sometimes comments that are intended to be supportive are interpreted by students as adding to pressure.

Resources

- The **help** you receive from friends, family, school, teachers, and other sources
  - Advice or explanation with your work
  - Belief in you / emotional support

- Your own **beliefs** about the importance of school, your ability, and effort or perseverance
  - "I am not very good at maths and so I have to try much harder than everyone else"
  - "I am not very good at maths so there Is not point trying"

Figure 3.9 This slide presents a couple of examples of perceived resources that are related to help from others or one's own self-beliefs such as self-confidence ("I am good at exams" and "I am good at maths"). These types of resources (actual or perceived) help the student feel that they are in a position to meet the challenge made by the demands. A critical point is that confidence does not go hand-in-hand with ability. Some students in high sets will not be confident in their ability and some students in low sets will be confident. This is partly because students judge their competence in particular subjects against their peers in the same class. A student who struggles in a high set may have lower confidence than a student in a lower set who does not struggle.

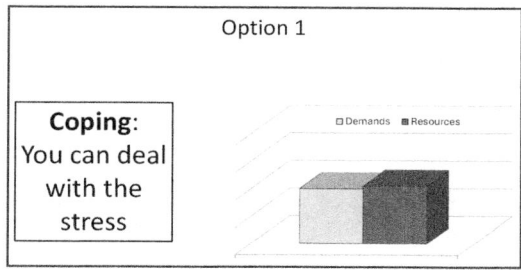

Figure 3.10 This slide presents the first of 3 options to illustrate different responses to stress. Option 1 is when demands and resources are roughly equal. The person can cope adequately with the level of demands placed on them (i.e., to use an analogy the person floats along, not sinking, but not swimming).

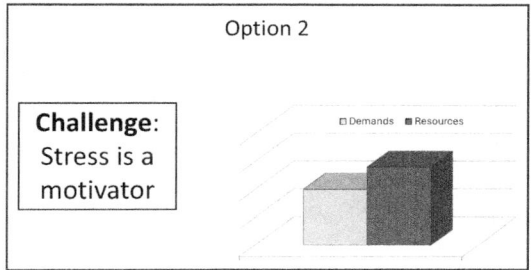

Figure 3.11 This slide presents the second of the three options; when resources outweigh demands. Demands are seen as a challenge that one is capable of meeting. Under these circumstances stress is a good thing and will drive people to achieve greater things than they would have without the stress.

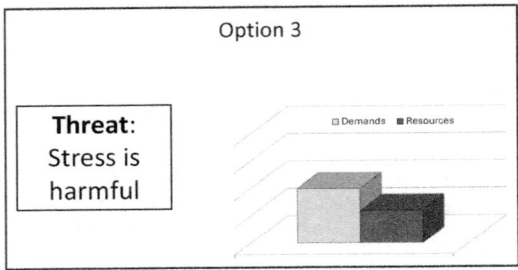

Figure 3.12 This presents the third of the three options; when demands outweigh resources. The person does not feel they are capable of meeting the demands made of them and they see the demand as a threat. This is when stress can become harmful and develop into exam anxiety.

CHAPTER SUMMARY

In this chapter, I have explained how exam anxiety can negatively impact achievement by interfering with information processing. Specifically, anxiety disrupts working memory processes and functions; the very processes and functions that are needed to perform well during exams. To a degree, the effects of anxiety can be offset with greater effort in exam preparation and by mobilising greater cognitive resources during an actual exam. However, the net effect is still negative. The belief that "a bit of stress can be a good thing" does have a grain of truth. Stress can assist performance when it results in a challenge state. Exam anxiety, however, results from a threat state, and the benefits from "a bit of anxiety" are minimal. Anything other than a small amount of anxiety will be damaging to performance; the more anxiety, the more damage. There are, however, ways to enable challenge rather than threat responses to pressure and I have briefly discussed some of the ways these can be incorporated into pedagogy and a motivational classroom atmosphere, as well as some ideas about how to discuss issues about exam stress with students.

NOTES

1 The majority of studies in this analysis were from the United States. For readers unfamiliar with their education system, compulsory education is referred to as K-12 (i.e., from kindergarten to grade 12). Grade 4 is the equivalent of year 5 in England and Wales, and Primary 6 in Northern Ireland and Scotland.
2 At the time when this study was conducted, GCSEs were awarded on an eight-point letter scale. A grade C was a minimum pass grade.
3 Year 6 National Curriculum Tests are taken at the end of primary school in England. The Cognitive Ability Test (CAT) is a standardised assessment of cognitive ability widely used in the UK published by Nelson.

4

HOW DOES EXAM ANXIETY RELATE TO MENTAL HEALTH AND WELL-BEING?

WHAT IS A MENTAL HEALTH DISORDER?

To gain a clear understanding of how exam anxiety differs from mental health disorders, it is first necessary to consider what mental health disorders refer to and the different ways in which mental disorders are understood. Like many specialist fields, mental health has its own distinct language drawn from medicine, epidemiology, and public health, and so I will introduce the key terms as we go along in italics. Traditionally, mental health disorders have been considered as analogous to physical health conditions in two ways. First, it is possible to create a taxonomy of mental health disorders (referred to as *nosological classification*). Second, different mental health disorders have distinct causes (referred to as *aetiology*), they develop differently and follow a different course, and they respond to different treatments. In some ways, these two points operate in a circular fashion, as the differentiation of one mental health condition from another can arise from an understanding of causes, development, courses, or outcomes.

The two most well-established nosological classification systems for mental health are the *International Classification of Diseases*, published by the World Health Organisation and presently in its 11th edition (ICD 11) and the *Diagnostic and Statistical Manual of*

Mental Disorders, published by the American Psychiatric Association and presently in its 5th edition with a subsequent text revision (DSM-5-TR). Each of these classification systems presents numerous distinguishable conditions, including those beginning early in life that are characterised by issues arising from the brain or nervous system and those where issues with brain function leads to problems with cognitive function and processing. A key distinction is between *internalising disorders,* where symptoms are expressed inwardly (e.g., sadness, anxiety, and loneliness), and *externalising disorders,* where symptoms are expressed outwardly (e.g., oppositional behaviours, antisocial behaviour, and relationship problems).

Although each of these groups of disorders is quite different, they are all marked by distress (to oneself or others), dysfunction (the person cannot function as they usually would do), danger (to oneself or others), and deviance (thoughts, emotions, or behaviours associated with poor mental health are uncommon). Within this classification, the various types of distinct *anxiety disorders* are considered a type of internalising disorder. Exam anxiety is not presently, nor has ever been, considered a distinct type of mental health disorder and is not listed in the DSM or ICD. The implication is that exam anxiety is perceived to be less serious than anxiety disorders (and other mental health conditions) and, therefore, less of a priority for assessment, identification, support, treatment, and resources.

EMOTION DISORDER

A survey conducted by NHS England, prior to the COVID pandemic showed that emotion disorder (an umbrella term for anxiety and mood disorders) was the most common mental health problem experienced in 11–19-year-olds (Vizard et al., 2018). Similar findings are reported in the United States (Bitsko et al., 2022) and worldwide (GBD 2019 Mental Disorders Collaborators, 2022). In Vizard et al.'s (2018) study, the most commonly experienced emotion disorders were *Major Depression*, followed by *Generalized Anxiety Disorder, Panic Disorder, Social Anxiety Disorder, Specific Phobia*, and *Separation Anxiety Disorder*. The major features of these disorders are listed in Table 4.1.

Table 4.1 *Characteristics of the Most Commonly Reported Emotion Disorders in England*

Disorder	Characteristics
Major depression	A depressed mood (e.g., feeling sad, empty, and hopeless), or a marked loss of interest and enjoyment in usual activities, over a discrete period; it can be accompanied by unexplained weight loss, fatigue and loss of energy, thoughts of death, suicidal ideation, or planning for suicide, and difficulty concentrating or making decisions.
Generalised anxiety disorder	Excessive and persistent worry (e.g., about work or school performance) that is difficult to control; it can be accompanied by restlessness, fatigue, muscle tension, irritability, and difficulty concentrating.
Panic disorder	Unexpected and recurrent bursts of intense fear and discomfort accompanied with physical symptoms such as heart palpitations, feelings of choking, nausea, dizziness, shortness of breath, and chest pain; worry about additional panic attacks and maladaptive changes in behaviour designed to avoid a panic attack (e.g., avoiding unfamiliar situations).
Social anxiety disorder	A persistent, intense, and disproportionate, fear of social situations where one can be scrutinised by others; worry that showing anxiety symptoms will result in embarrassment or rejection by others; social situations are avoided or endured with extreme discomfort. Examples of social situations include interactions with others, being observed, and performing in front of others.
Specific phobia	A persistent, intense, and disproportionate, fear of specific object or situation (e.g., flying, heights, animals, injections, seeing blood); phobic objects or situations are avoided or endured with extreme discomfort; the fear or avoidance causes distress and impairment in other areas of functioning (e.g., social and work).
Separation anxiety disorder	Inappropriate and excessive fear of separation from those to whom an individual is attached; it can be accompanied by intense distress when anticipating separation, persistent refusal to leave home, attend school or work out of a fear of separation, and physical symptoms (e.g., headaches, nausea, and stomach-aches) when separation occurs or is anticipated.

WHAT IS THE DIFFERENCE BETWEEN TEST ANXIETY AND MENTAL HEALTH DISORDERS?

If we compare the characteristics of the common emotion disorders presented in Table 4.1 to the cognitive and affective-physiological signs of exam anxiety shown in Box 1.1 (see Chapter 1), it is possible to see overlaps and similarities. Generalised Anxiety Disorder is characterised by uncontrollable worries which, for children and adolescents, can be about school performance. Exam anxiety is also characterised by worry about school performance, although specifically in relation to test and exam performance. In addition, Generalised Anxiety Disorder can be accompanied by muscle tension which is one of the affective-physiological signs of exam anxiety. Both Generalised Anxiety Disorder and Major Depression can be accompanied by difficulty in concentration, which is also a cognitive sign of exam anxiety (specifically that of cognitive interference). The physical symptoms that accompany Panic Disorder (e.g., heart palpitations, nausea, and dizziness) mirror the physiological elements of exam anxiety.

One situation in which Social Anxiety can manifest is where a person's performance is observed by others. Such situations can be encountered where subjects include an examined performance element (e.g., music or drama). We can distinguish social from exam anxiety as the former presents a threat to one's social competence, whereas the latter is a threat to one's academic competence (see Chapter 1). In written exams, performance is not directly assessed during the examination period itself (they are marked later on).

Nonetheless, a student could still fear that their behaviour could be scrutinised by others (e.g., other students in the same exam or the invigilator). In addition, exam situations could become one of the situations in which a phobic response develops. Moreover, Panic Disorder, Social Anxiety, and Specific Phobia, can all be accompanied by avoidance. As I briefly described in Chapter 1, exam anxiety can also motivate students to avoid situations that require them to think about exams, such as planning and undertaking exam preparation. It is only Separation Anxiety Disorder which does not show an obvious overlap with exam anxiety.

As exam anxiety seems to overlap with characteristics of common anxiety disorders one may wonder exactly why exam anxiety is not classified as a mental disorder while the other disorders are. There is no simple and straightforward reason for this. One argument is that that for a person to be diagnosed with an emotion disorder they have to not only display the symptoms of that disorder, but that the symptoms result in a significant degree of distress and dysfunction to one's life. There may be a perception that the level of distress and dysfunction associated with exam anxiety is not as severe as that of emotion disorder. This argument is not, however, supported by data. In Chapter 2, I briefly discussed how students can report severe levels of distress in relation to exam anxiety and at high levels, exam anxiety may be associated with the presence of anxiety disorders (von der Embse et al., 2021). I will expand on this idea in the section that follows and review studies showing that persons reporting high levels of exam anxiety meet diagnostic thresholds for anxiety disorders.

A second argument is that emotion disorder is diagnosed as present or absent (i.e., one is diagnosed with the disorder or not), whereas exam anxiety is continuous; that is, a person can show varying degrees of exam anxiety ranging from very little to moderate to severe. This is also an idea we touched on in Chapter 2 when considering the "How Many?" question (see Figure 2.1). However, the categorical approach to the diagnosis of mental disorders is not without criticism. Persons who do not meet a diagnostic threshold for an anxiety disorder may still experience significant distress and dysfunction, and require support or treatment (Bosman et al., 2019). That is, mental health conditions are not an all or nothing phenomenon.

The alternative to a categorical classification approach is referred to as *dimensional* whereby the frequency and severity of symptoms are assessed. Support and/or treatment are then considered proportionally to the level of distress and dysfunction. Although DSM-5-TR (and its predecessor, DSM-5) maintains an emphasis on categorical diagnosis, a simultaneous dimensional assessment of disorders is encouraged (Helzer et al., 2007). It would be prudent not to rule out exam anxiety as a mental health condition purely because it is not presently categorised as one.

A third argument, advanced when DSM-5 was being developed, is that a person who showed anxiety in exam situations could already be diagnosed with an existing disorder (LeBeau et al., 2010). This position does not diminish the distress associated with high levels of exam anxiety, rather exam anxiety is being treated as a symptom of an existing disorder. However, along with criticism of a categorical approach to diagnosis, the traditional nosological classification of mental disorders has also been criticised due to *comorbidity*. This is where a person with one condition simultaneously shows symptoms of additional conditions, and many conditions share similar causes, develop outcomes, and also respond to similar treatments (Dalgeish et al., 2020). These areas of similarity undermine the distinction between one disorder and another, especially so when the presence of one disorder overlaps with the presence of another. This would imply that, perhaps, they are different manifestations of a broader condition.

This is particularly the case with emotion disorders which undermines the validity of a taxonomic system that differentiates between different types of anxiety and mood disorders. The alternative is a *transdiagnostic* approach whereby an assessment is made on the basis of symptoms that transcend traditional taxonomic classifications of mental disorders. For the transdiagnostic approach the critical issue is the symptoms that are shown by a person, and how they can be treated, rather than the label assigned to those conditions. In the approach advocated by Tim Dalgeish and colleagues (2020), for example, symptoms of internalising disorders (including sexual problems, eating pathology, fear, distress, and mania) are likely to overlap to a greater or lesser extent. From this perspective, it does not matter that exam anxiety is, or was, not a recognised mental health condition in DSM or the ICD. The critical issue is the symptoms shown by the person (e.g., fear and distress) and the extent to which those impact the person.

A study by Gabrielle Yale-Soulière and colleagues (2024) asked adolescent students, aged 15–18 years to complete standardised measures of test anxiety, Generalised Anxiety Disorder, Social Anxiety Disorder, and Panic Disorder. A relatively complex analysis[1] was used to establish whether exam anxiety, and symptoms of the three anxiety disorders, could be cleanly separated. Results showed that while there were unique features for all four types of anxiety, they were *all* underpinned by a general propensity to experience anxiety. The implication is that there is a common element to both exam anxiety and clinical anxiety disorders which likely results from the same mechanisms. These findings support adopting a transdiagnostic approach to exam anxiety and anxiety disorders.

What are we to make of these complex ideas and debates? Pinning down the exact difference between exam anxiety and mental health disorders (especially those characterised by fear and anxiety) is not straightforward. The further we dig down into the differences, the harder it becomes to clearly differentiate exam anxiety from anxiety disorders more generally. One might reasonably ask if it really matters whether exam anxiety is aligned with mental health conditions or not? I believe that it does for two reasons. First, it emphasises the degree of distress and dysfunction experienced by some students before and during exams. This makes it harder to dismiss exam anxiety as trivial and reinforces the distinction from stress (see Chapter 3). Second, access to support or intervention, exam accommodations, or the resources to provide these, may depend on the recognition of poor mental health.

ARE SEVERELY EXAM-ANXIOUS STUDENTS AT RISK OF POOR MENTAL HEALTH?

Several studies have addressed this question in different ways. One type of study examines whether severely exam-anxious students meet the diagnostic criteria for a mental health disorder, such as those listed in Table 4.1. The second is whether severely exam-anxious students also report more frequent or intense symptoms of mental health disorders. The first type of study might be considered more objective in that the diagnosis is made by a clinician (either a clinical psychologist or a psychiatrist), while the second approach aligns with a more dimensional approach to diagnosis. I will provide two examples of each type of study.

An example of the first type of study was conducted in Australia by Neville King and colleagues (1995). Six hundred grade 9 and 10 students (corresponding to Years 10 and 11 in England and Wales; Years 11 and 12 in Northern Ireland) completed the Test Anxiety Scale for Children (TASC: which comprises 30 yes/no questions). The top 5% of scores (30 students) was treated as the exam-anxious group and the bottom 5% of scores (also 30 students) was treated as the non-exam-anxious group. Eighteen of the exam-anxious group agreed to participate in a diagnostic interview (using an earlier version of the DSM) and 11 were diagnosed with an anxiety disorder (61%). Twenty-five of the non-exam-anxious group agreed to participate in a diagnostic interview and 2 were diagnosed with an anxiety disorder (8%).

Of the exam-anxious group, nine were diagnosed with *Overanxious Disorder* (a disorder characterised by excessive and persistent worry about competence (e.g., academic) accompanied by tension, and physical symptoms (e.g., stomach-ache and headaches) that was subsequently incorporated into Generalised Anxiety Disorder in later versions of the DSM), seven with Separation Anxiety Disorder, four with Specific Phobia (referred to as *Simple Phobia* at the time), and three with *Avoidant Disorder of Childhood and Adolescence* (a disorder characterised by withdrawal from social contact with unfamiliar persons and a desire for social involvement with familiar persons, subsequently incorporated into Social Anxiety in later versions of the DSM). Seven persons received multiple diagnoses (i.e., comorbidity).

A second example of this type of study was conducted in Germany by, Frank Herzer and colleagues (2014). They followed 45 adult students (the clinical sample) with a forthcoming test who had self-referred themselves to the university outpatient clinic. Following a diagnostic interview, 23 were diagnosed with Specific Phobia, 11 with Social Anxiety, and six with Major Depression or *Dysthymia* (persistent depression); 22 received two, and 7 three, comorbid diagnoses (most commonly, Major Depression and Specific Phobia). This clinical sample was compared to a group of 41 adult students, matched for age and level of education, who showed no sign of a mental disorder (confirmed with a diagnostic interview). Both the clinical sample and the comparison group completed the German version of the Test Anxiety Inventory (comprising 30 questions on a four-point scale resulting in a score from 30 to 120). A score of 80 (i.e., the 66th scale percentile) correctly identified 100% of the comparison group (i.e., they all scored less than 80) and 93.6% of the clinical group (i.e., all but 2 scored 80 or higher).

An example of the second type of study was conducted in the United States by Margaret Warren and colleagues (1996). They asked 446 students from grades 4, 7, and 10 (corresponding to Years 5, 8, and 11, in England and Wales; Years 6, 9, and 12 in Northern Ireland), to complete the Test Anxiety Inventory (briefly described in Chapter 2) alongside measures for anxiety and depression symptoms. The upper tertile (33%) of scores were treated as highly exam-anxious and the lower tertile as low exam-anxious. This resulted in 156 exam-anxious students (99 girls and 57 boys) and 152 non-exam-anxious students (91 boys and 62 girls).

In order to gauge the differences in anxiety and depression symptoms between the exam-anxious and non-anxious groups, we can make use of a statistic called the Cohen's *d* effect size. Cohen's *d* represents the difference in scores (anxiety and depression symptoms in this case) between two groups in a standardised form; that is, it does not matter what the original scale was measured on (e.g., 20–60, or 30–120). A rule of thumb for interpreting Cohen's *d* is that if the value is less than 0.2 means the difference between two groups is very small, 0.2–0.5 is small, 0.5–0.8 is moderate, 0.8–1.20 is large, 1.20–2.0 is very large, and greater than

2.0 is huge (Sawilowsky, 2009). The exam-anxious group reported stronger anxiety symptoms that ranged from moderate to huge ($ds = 0.72–2.67$) and stronger depression symptoms that ranged from moderate to very large ($ds = 0.57–1.88$).[2]

In a second study of this type, also from the United States, Carl Weems and colleagues (2014) asked 202 4th and 8th graders (corresponding to Years 5 and 9, in England and Wales; Years 6 and 10 in Northern Ireland) to complete an 18-item version of the TASC along with measures of symptoms for Generalised Anxiety Disorder, Social Anxiety, Panic Disorder, Separation Anxiety Disorder, and Major Depression. Students who scored 8 or higher on the TASC (i.e., the 44th scale percentile) were treated as the exam-anxious group, and those below as the non-exam-anxious group. The exam-anxious group reported moderately higher symptoms for the aforementioned anxiety disorders ($ds = .71–.95$) and Major Depression ($d = .86$) than the non-anxious group.

These studies indicate that highly exam-anxious students report stronger (i.e., more frequent and intense) symptoms for anxiety and depression and are more likely to meet the threshold for an anxiety disorder and/or Major Depression, than students who are less exam-anxious. The cut-point used to establish 'high' exam anxiety in these four studies was arbitrary and differed from one study to the next. This creates a problem when trying to establish the score, or range of scores, on an exam anxiety scale that indicates elevated symptoms of an emotion disorder. That is, although persons with higher exam anxiety also show symptoms (either self-reported or diagnosed) of mental health conditions, it is less clear exactly where the tipping point lies.

Alongside studies linking exam anxiety to mental disorder diagnoses and symptoms are those of a more epidemiological nature that link exam pressures to indicators of poor mental health. In one study of this type, Kathryn Beck and colleagues (2024) in a sample of 18,052 Norwegian students aged 17–21 years, found that those who failed a high-stakes upper-secondary school exit exam (equivalent to A Levels), were more likely to receive a diagnosis related to poor mental health from a primary-care physician (e.g., anxiety, depression, and alcohol abuse) in the following 12-month period.

In another study of this type, Björn Högberg and colleagues (2020) used data from the World Health Organisation's Health Behaviours of School-Aged Children (HBSC) survey to show, in a sample of 29,199 Swedish students aged 11–16 years, to show that school stress related to a range of psychological and physical health complaints include headache, stomach-ache, dizziness, backache, sleeping difficulties, feeling low, nervous, and irritable or bad tempered mood. In addition, the contribution of school stress to psychological and physical health complaints increased over time (the authors examined data from 1993 to 2017) and girls were more adversely affected.

An important point, however, is that a characteristic of a mental health disorder is deviance; that is, the presence of symptoms is statistically unlikely (even for 'common' conditions). If severe exam anxiety was common, then it would not be statistically deviant and hence should not be considered as a mental health disorder in its own right or as a symptom of another condition (Lovett et al., 2024). The studies I reviewed in Chapter 2 (the "how many?" question) lend support to this view, although it should be recalled that there is no agreed threshold for what constitutes 'severe' exam anxiety, and many studies adopt an arbitrary approach. This point is not intended to undermine the distress experienced by severely exam-anxious persons, or to weaken the case for support and/or intervention. Rather, it is just that if exam anxiety is common, it is not a mental health condition.

Indeed, Benjamin Lovett argues exam anxiety can be a rational response to failure in high-stakes settings. I am sceptical of this argument for two reasons. First, it does not sit well with individual differences in exam anxiety (see Figure 2.1); are those who are less anxious also less rational? Second, there are certain types of thinking (for instance, like perfectionist "all or nothing" thinking) that exaggerate and magnify what might be otherwise manageable fears about one's academic competence. These types of thinking (referred to cognitive *biases* or *distortions*) are the very same ones that also lead to other emotion disorders like Generalised Anxiety Disorder, Panic Disorder, and Major Depression. This is an idea that we shall return to in Chapter 5.

In addition, because high exam anxiety coincides with symptoms and/or diagnosis of a mental health condition does not necessarily mean exam anxiety is a risk for poor mental health. In fact, it could be that it is those persons who already have elevated symptoms and/or diagnosis of a mental health condition who are becoming more exam-anxious. This is a classic "chicken and egg" conundrum encountered in research based on naturalistic data. When two things (like exam anxiety and elevated symptoms of a mental health condition) coincide (or to use statistical parlance, *correlate*), it is difficult to determine which causes which, or whether they are both the result of another variable (or variables).

To pick up on a theme I introduced in Chapter 3 when considering how exam anxiety is related to achievement, the only way to establish definitively if exam anxiety is causing elevated symptoms of a mental health condition is to experimentally manipulate exam anxiety (i.e., deliberately make some students exam-anxious) to see what happens to their mental health. Clearly this is not a practical or ethical option. However, if we measured exam anxiety and elevated symptoms of a mental health condition on two or more occasions, with a time lag in between, we could see whether higher exam anxiety followed elevated symptoms of a mental health condition, elevated symptoms of a mental health condition followed higher exam anxiety, or a combination of the two. In statistical parlance we could establish *directionality*.

In the only study of this type to have been conducted, this far, my colleagues and I collected data from 1198 English Year 12 students (Putwain, Gallard, et al., 2021) over two waves. The first wave of data collection was in October (in England, the school year starts in September), and the second was in May of the following year (the same school year). Participants were asked to report their exam anxiety and the Academic and Emotional Risk Screener from which their risk of developing an emotion disorder was inferred (labelled emotion risk). In addition, participants were asked to report their subjective well-being at school (I will explain more about different approaches to well-being later in this chapter). The results are summarised in Figure 4.1.

The dashed lines refer to the correlations between exam anxiety, well-being, and emotion risk, at the first (T1) and second (T2) waves of data collection. In methodological parlance, these are referred to as concurrent (or unlagged, i.e., no time lag) relations. A positive value refers to a positive correlation. For example, the correlation of .45 between exam anxiety and emotion risk at T1 indicates that they are positively correlated; as exam anxiety scores increase, so do those for emotion risk (and vice versa). A negative value refers to a negative correlation. For example, the correlation of −.20 between exam anxiety and well-being at T2 indicates that as exam anxiety scores increase, well-being scores decrease (and vice versa). Just as there are rules of thumb for interpreting effect sizes, there are also rules of thumb for interpreting correlations. Irrespective of whether the correlation is positive or negative, those below .1 are considered

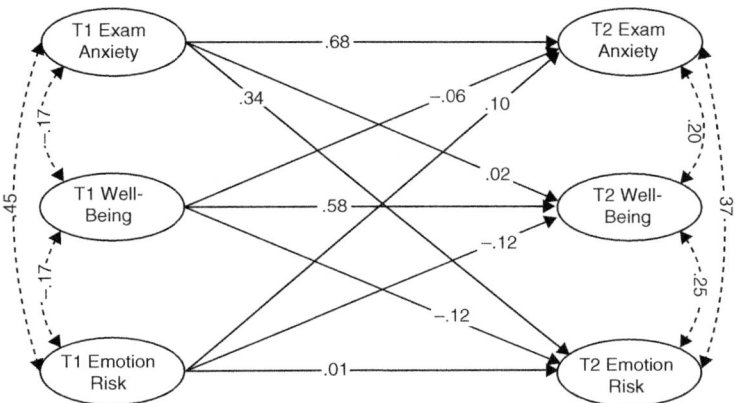

Figure 4.1 Relations Between Exam Anxiety, Well-Being, and Emotion Risk Over Two Waves of Data Collection.

Source: Adapted from Putwain, Gallard et al. (2021), p. 1156.

as negligible, those from .1 to .3 as small, those from .3 to .5 as moderate, and above .5 as large (Cohen, 1988). Accordingly, we could say there was a moderate positive correlation between exam anxiety and emotion risk at T1 and a small negative correlation between exam anxiety and well-being at T2.

The solid straight lines from T1 to T2 exam anxiety and well-being refer to the stability of scores from October to May. Unlike the dashed correlations, these *paths* have only arrows at one end to indicate their directionality; only scores at T1 can predict scores at T2, not vice versa. These are called auto-lagged or auto-regressive paths. The values presented on those lines are a type of statistic called a standardised regression, or beta, coefficient (β). Rules of thumb for their interpretation are that from .05 to .09 βs are small, from .10 to .24 as moderate, and greater than .25 as large (Keith, 2015). The coefficients of .68, for exam anxiety, and .58 for well-being, indicate a strong relation between scores at T1 and T2 (i.e., scores were highly stable). The coefficient of .01 for T1 to T2 emotion risk indicates that there was no stability in scores over time. This is most likely as participants were instructed to report their emotion risk for the preceding four weeks only, not how they felt more generally.

The diagonal solid back lines are called cross-lagged paths and are also beta coefficients. The strength of this type of statistical modelling is that we can be sure that any cross-lagged relations we observe are not an artefact of variables being correlated (either at T1 or T2) or stable over time. In statistical parlance, we have *controlled* for concurrent and auto-regressive relations. Having controlled for concurrent relations and stability in scores over time, T1 exam anxiety was a strong predictor (β = .34) of T2 emotion risk, whereas T1 emotion risk was a moderate predictor (β = .10) of T2 exam anxiety. We can conclude, therefore, that exam anxiety *is* a risk for subsequently developing an emotion disorder. Persons with an elevated risk for developing an emotion disorder are also at risk for becoming more exam-anxious. The risk is bidirectional (or reciprocally related). However, relations from exam anxiety to emotion risk were much larger than from emotion risk to exam anxiety; the risk is not equal.

The model also included cross-lagged paths for well-being. Higher T1 well-being was a small predictor of lower T2 exam anxiety ($\beta = -.06$) and a moderate predictor of lower T2 emotion risk ($\beta = -.12$). Higher T1 emotion risk was also a small predictor of lower T2 well-being ($\beta = -.12$), but not exam anxiety ($\beta = .02$). Therefore, we can conclude that well-being and emotion risk are bidirectional. Well-being and exam anxiety, however, were not. Higher well-being predicted lower subsequent exam anxiety but not vice versa. This study leads nicely onto the final section of this chapter in which I will consider the relation between exam anxiety and well-being in more detail.

DOES EXAM ANXIETY UNDERMINE WELL-BEING?

Well-being is a term that is often used in a loose and hazy fashion. When it comes to examining how well-being relates to other psychological (e.g., exam anxiety) and educational (e.g., achievement) phenomena, this lack of precision is not helpful; what exactly does well-being refer to (or not)? In addition, well-being is sometimes accompanied by adjectives such as *mental* well-being or *emotional* well-being. Again, this is not helpful. Is mental well-being, for example, the same as the absence of a mental health condition or does it imply the presence of something and, if so, what? Is emotional well-being just a proxy for the absence of negative emotions and the presence of positive emotions; or is it how one regulates and deals with negative emotions that arise in difficult, aversive, or adverse, circumstances?

It is, therefore, important to define well-being clearly. A common distinction, drawn from origins in Greek philosophy is the distinction between eudaimonic and hedonic well-being (Ryan & Deci, 2001). Hedonic, or subjective, well-being comprises life satisfaction together with the presence of positive mood and the absence of negative mood. Broadly speaking, this might described as happiness. Furthermore, subjective well-being can be considered in relation to one's life as a whole or specific domains of one's life (e.g., school, family, friends, work, and so on). If we are investigating subjective well-being in relation to educational, or school-related, issues (like exam anxiety or achievement), I would argue that it is more sensitive, precise, and meaningful to specifically measure school-related well-being rather than general well-being.

If a student was highly anxious about exams, but not anxious in other areas of their life, she or he might report average, or even low, scores on a general measure of anxiety. A general measure of anxiety, therefore, would be insufficiently sensitive to accurately measure exam anxiety specifically. In a similar way, a student may have high school-related well-being, but not in other areas of their life. She or he might, therefore, report an average level of well-being overall; such an approach is not sufficiently sensitive to accurately measure well-being at school. The consequence would be to underestimate the relations between how well-being and other educational or school-related issues.

An alternative, eudaimonic approach to well-being is finding meaning and purpose in one's life and comprises elements of personal growth, environmental mastery, positive relationships, autonomy, and self-actualisation. One can see obvious links to education here, where individuals are able to follow and use their passions and interests to pursue a meaningful life. Of course, these different elements of well-being are not necessarily distinct. From one perspective, eudaimonic well-being could be viewed as the antecedents of well-being, and hedonic well-being, as the outcome (Diener et al., 2018).

Just like the terms exam stress and anxiety are used interchangeably (see Chapter 1) but do not necessarily refer to the same thing, well-being is often used interchangeably with mental health. We can pose the same question here; is well-being the same as mental health? If we consider the different perspectives on well-being, would either hedonic or eudaimonic well-being guarantee the presence of mental health, or put another way, the absence of a mental health condition?

Shannon Suldo has developed a framework, referred to as the "Dual Factor Model" (Suldo et al., 2018), for thinking about this question. The central idea is that the presence of a mental health condition will likely contribute to lower subjective well-being, for instance, through negative emotions (especially in the case of mood disorders) and interfering with activities that bring one happiness. However, there could be other elements of one's life (e.g., trusting and supportive relationships, along with activities that a mental health condition does not impact) that maintain subjective well-being. In short, the presence of a mental health condition does not guarantee low well-being. Similarly, the absence of a mental health condition does not guarantee high subjective well-being if there are elements of one's life that are problematic (e.g., relationships and school, or work problems). From this perspective complete mental health requires both the presence of subjective well-being *and* the absence of a mental health condition. The implication of this perspective is than well-being cannot be used as a proxy for good mental health (or the absence of a mental health condition).

This distinction was the premise for the study I described above (see Figure 4.1) that included both well-being (incidentally, this was school-specific subjective well-being) and the risk for emotion disorder as distinct variables. In addition to this study (Putwain, Gallard, et al., 2021), several others have shown that exam anxiety is negatively correlated with school-related subjective well-being. That is, higher exam anxiety is associated with lower well-being (Putwain, von der Emsbe, 2021). Of course, correlations will always pose a chicken and egg question. Is the higher exam anxiety contributing to the lower well-being or vice versa?

Somewhat surprisingly, in my 2021 study (Putwain, Gallard, et al., 2021) when risk for emotion disorder was accounted for, along with the concurrent relations between exam anxiety and the stability of exam anxiety over time, exam anxiety *did not* contribute to lower subsequent subjective well-being. Students who already had low subjective well-being at T1 did report higher exam anxiety at T2, but the contribution was small. It may be the case that while the negative emotional state associated with exam anxiety could contribute to lower subjective well-being at school, there are other aspects of school life that maintain well-being (e.g., supporting and trusting relationships with peers and teachers).

Another study to examine the directionality between exam anxiety and subjective well-being, alongside achievement, was conducted in Germany by Ricarda Steinmayr and colleagues (2016). Over two measurement points, one year apart, 11th grade students[3] reported two elements of exam anxiety (separate worry and affective-physiological components) and their generic (not school-specific) subjective well-being (separate mood and life satisfaction components). After controlling for concurrent correlations, and stability over time, the worry component of exam anxiety at T1 predicted lower mood, life satisfaction, and achievement, at T2. Well-being at T1, however, was unrelated to exam anxiety at T2.

It is not easy to pinpoint why my study did not show that exam anxiety negatively impacted well-being but Ricarda's did. We approached well-being in different ways (I measured school-specific with a single dimension, whereas she measured generic well-being with two dimensions) and included different constructs alongside exam anxiety and well-being (I included emotion risk and she included achievement). Both could have had an influence. Until further studies are conducted, and we have more evidence, I think the prudent conclusion would be simply that we know that higher exam anxiety and lower well-being are related. However, we cannot say with certainty that it is the higher exam anxiety *leading* to the lower well-being rather than vice versa.

CHAPTER SUMMARY

In this chapter, I had considered the evidence linking exam anxiety to mental health and well-being. This is not a straightforward task due to debates and critiques over how mental health is classified and diagnosed, and how well-being is defined. Accordingly, to lead the reader through these, often complex, issues and debates, it was necessary to set out terms, definitions, and contested meanings. I am mindful that parts of this chapter are quite dense as we work through them, but my hope is that by doing so the reader will be in a more informed position to judge the studies I describe. I suggest three conclusions are plausible. First, high test anxiety is associated with elevated symptoms of some mental disorders (notably anxiety disorders and depression) and lower subjective well-being. Second, whether exam anxiety constitutes a mental disorder, a symptom of a disorder, or a risk for a disorder, depends on the approach to the classification and diagnosis of mental disorders. Third, on the available evidence, we cannot conclude at present that exam anxiety undermines well-being.

NOTES

1   A bifactor exploratory structural equation model (B-ESEM).
2   Although effect size statistics were not reported in this study, I calculated Cohen's *d*s from the means and SDs.
3   In Germany, the age at which children start school varies from one state to another. In this study, the mean age of students was 16.5 years on the first measurement occasion making this the equivalent of Year 12 in England and Wales and Year 13 in Northern Ireland).

5

HOW DOES EXAM ANXIETY ARISE

WHERE DOES IT COME FROM?

THE SELF-REFERENT EXECUTIVE FUNCTION MODEL

The Self-Referent Executive Function (S-REF) model (Wells & Matthews, 1994, 1996) was originally developed as an explanation for how inflexible and ruminative styles of thinking about negative beliefs, feelings, and thoughts, later termed the *Cognitive Attentional Syndrome* (CAS; Wells, 2009), underpin the distress associated with emotion disorder (i.e., anxiety and depression). CAS comprises the use of ineffective coping strategies (e.g., thought suppression, avoidance, and rumination) resulting from metacognitive beliefs about anxiety. The S-REF model has subsequently been applied to post-traumatic stress, problematic gambling and alcohol use, and extended to a number of evaluation-related anxieties, including exam anxiety, by Moshe Ziedner and Gerald Matthews (2005). In this first section of Chapter 5, I will introduce the S-REF model more generally, including some of the assumptions and key terms. I will follow this in the second section of this chapter by drawing on Zeidner and Matthews' application of the S-REF model to explain how exam anxiety is developed and maintained.

DOI: 10.4324/9781032716411-5

By proposing a common CAS that underpins different mental health problems characterised by emotional distress and maladaptive behaviours, the S-REF model aligns with a transdiagnostic approach to mental disorders. This is an idea I touched on in Chapter 4 and one of the principal reasons why I am drawn to the S-REF model as an explanation for exam anxiety. That is, the same processes that lead to other forms of anxiety and emotional distress also lead to exam anxiety. We can sidestep complex arguments about whether exam anxiety should, or should not, be considered as a mental disorder and focus on the processes that lead to distress and, by implication, what can be done about it.

The architecture of the S-REF (Figure 5.1) is based on three interacting information-processing systems. The first system comprises automatic processing of information which requires little or no conscious attention or effort (a *stimulus-driven processing network*). The second system is based on the conscious and deliberate processing of information which is attentionally demanding and requires effort (*executive processes*). The third system comprises *self-knowledge*. This includes beliefs about oneself (e.g., "Unless I should be succeed and achieve at whatever I do, making no mistakes, I am worthless") and generic plans for dealing with motivationally salient events, such as a forthcoming exam that is judged to be important. A generic plan could be, for instance, to cope by using avoidance-based strategies (e.g., distraction from worry) or task-focusing strategies (e.g., expending effort in exam preparation).

The stimulus-driven processing network screens events to determine whether they require conscious attention or not based on simplified self-knowledge beliefs (e.g., a person's values, goals, and needs) and operates on the edge of, or under, conscious awareness (i.e., the person is not or may be only vaguely aware of them). If a person's simplified self-knowledge beliefs include perfectionist thoughts like the one mentioned above ("Unless I achieve and make no mistakes, I am a failure") any event that evaluates achievement could result in thoughts (e.g., worry), feelings (e.g., panic), and physiological responses (e.g., elevated heart rate), that impinge into conscious awareness (hence the person becomes aware of them). Executive processes are triggered by such intrusions into conscious awareness, as well as those events themselves that are motivationally charged.

Executive processing involves the intentional processing of event appraisals (e.g., "how important is this to me?") and available options to cope with the event that are influenced by metacognitive processes (metacognitive knowledge, control, and monitoring). Executive processes influence how a student would, for instance, focus and direct attention, filter distractions, set and achieve goals, and control impulses. Executive processes draw on self-knowledge beliefs to determine the importance of the event and how one should cope with it, and generic plans are modified in accordance with the demands of the specific situation.

Positive self-beliefs (e.g., "I am good at maths") and generic plans that are adaptive (e.g., to use task-focused strategies) might prompt the person to formulate a specific study plan and what that might involve, such as what exam topics need to be revised, when to revise, what study strategies to use, what practice questions to try, and so on. In this case, the episode of executive processing could be fairly brief, and attention can be focused onto other matters, like the exam preparation. Ongoing monitoring of the exam preparation will return to the stimulus-driven processing network and future executive processing will be triggered only if there is a subsequent discrepancy between the situation and one's goals (e.g., a person had to miss a planned period of exam study and needs to replan where to fit in the missing session).

The CAS describes how metacognitive knowledge, monitoring, and control, result in ineffective coping strategies and ongoing executive processes that maintain anxiety. Metacognitive knowledge, in this context, refers to beliefs a person holds about worry. According to Wells (2009) a person can hold positive or negative metacognitive beliefs about worry. A negative metacognitive belief, for instance, is that worry is uncontrollable, such as that once it has started it will never stop. If a person believes that worry cannot be controlled, they will invest little effort in disrupting it, and the worry will persist. However, a positive metacognitive belief about worry might be that worrying can help avoid future problems (e.g., worrying about a situation might help come up with a solution). Such a belief results in failure to interrupt the worry and using metacognitive control to intensify the worry.

The metacognitive monitoring and control strategies described here also sensitise the flow of information from the stimulus-driven processing network to executive processes. This may take the form of being vigilant for cues in situations and events related to one's worries (such as evaluative events) and more intensive monitoring of one's internal state. Such vigilance is attentionally demanding and, as we saw from Eysenck's attention control theory in Chapter 3, can interfere with learning and achievement. Although metacognitive beliefs can be distinguished by their valence, this solely refers to a person's beliefs about anxiety and not to whether those beliefs result in positive or negative outcomes. Both positive and negative metacognitive beliefs can maintain and exaggerate anxiety and from that perspective, both are related to pejorative outcomes.

S-REF processing can also result in maladaptive interactions with situations and persons. A common form of coping with anxiety is avoidance of the anxiety-provoking situation. Other coping strategies could involve *safety behaviours* that are designed to prevent a 'catastrophic' outcome (e.g., "If I fail an exam, my whole life will be a failure"). This could mean, for instance, a student going to the opposite extreme and spending so much time studying for an exam that it is to the detriment of their health. If the catastrophic outcome did not occur (i.e., the desired grade was achieved), the likelihood of the catastrophic outcome is never challenged, and hence, the safety behaviour is reinforced, and the threat status of events and situations involving exams never changes. These potentially harmful behaviours would persist the next time the student encounters a similar situation.

THE S-REF MODEL OF EXAM ANXIETY

As I mentioned earlier, the S-REF model was extended to include evaluation anxieties by Zeidner and Matthews (2005) and is shown in Figure 5.1. The starting point of the model is a potential situational threat such as a forthcoming exam. Threat cues could be external or situational (e.g., a teacher discussing what topics will be covered on that exam) or an internal cue (e.g., the student remembering they have a forthcoming exam). Although the stimulus-driven processing network is not explicitly emphasised in Figure 5.1, the level of threat would be initially determined automatically when exam success or failure would have significant consequences for one's goals, values, and needs. This would be the case when, for instance, a student has strongly internalised the value of academic credentials and bases their self-worth on academic success. It would also occur when a student believed they would be judged harshly by key others (e.g., family members, peers, or teachers) on academic success (or failure), or if a student strongly aspired to follow a particular educational or training route that required certain grades.

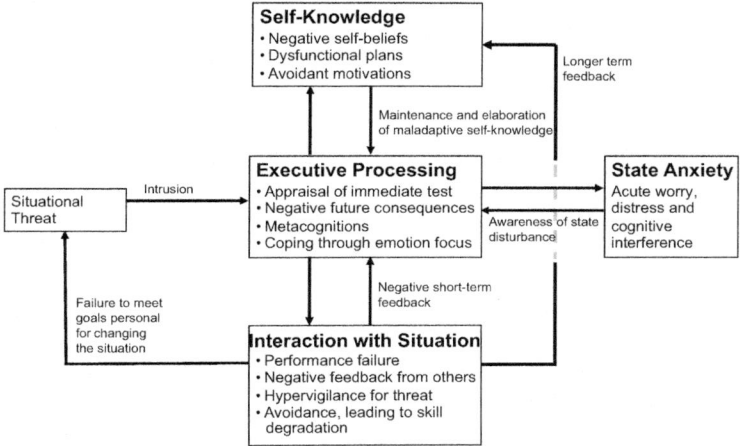

Figure 5.1 Zeidner and Matthews' S-REF model of Evaluation Anxiety.
Source: Zeidner and Matthews (2005, p. 154).

AUTOMATIC STIMULUS-DRIVE PROCESSING

As the stimulus-driven process network is a largely automated process, the person may be only partly or vaguely aware of the threat which may take the form of automatic negative thoughts, first described by Aaron Beck (1979) in his influential cognitive theory of emotion disorder. These are self-critical, biased, unrealistic, and self-defeating thoughts that occur quickly and at the edge of conscious awareness such as "I am bound to fail", "what is the point of trying, I will never pass", or "unless I receive a top grade, I am a failure". Automatic negative thoughts arise from negative core self-knowledge beliefs. The latter example might arise from the perfectionist thought "unless I achieve and succeed at whatever I do, making no mistakes, I am worthless".

SELF-KNOWLEDGE BELIEFS

Awareness of the forthcoming exam itself as well, as automatic negative thoughts and their associated worries (e.g., about failure), feelings (e.g., anxiety), and physiological responses (e.g., stomach discomfort) that intrude into conscious awareness will trigger executive processes. Executive processes will involve a fully conscious appraisal of the situation, the likelihood of and implications of success and failure, and what can be done about it. These appraisals will draw on self-knowledge beliefs and generic plans for action. Persons who become highly anxious about exams will typically draw on self-beliefs that emphasise the importance of success and failure (e.g., "I need a high grade to be accepted on my university course" or "If I fail this exam, it will mean I am worthless") and about one's competence (e.g., "I am no good at exams" or "I am no good at History"). These self-beliefs that emphasise the importance of the exam, along with uncertain success, will result in an appraisal of the exam as being threatening.

Generic plans for action could be focused on options to avoid or control feelings of anxiety, or to expend effort in exam preparation to reduce the likelihood of failure. For students with negative competence self-beliefs, plans to avoid or control anxiety may be more likely. However, students with high competence beliefs could still become highly anxious if they held strong perfectionist self-beliefs that anything other than the highest grade would be considered a failure. These students may be more likely to access plans to engage in excessive exam preparation. From one perspective, it could be questioned whether the latter approach is a problem. Such students may end up as high academic achievers and enjoy subsequent successful careers.

My solution is that we judge the extent to which the perfectionist belief has become detrimental to the student's usual functioning and well-being. If the student is putting extreme pressure on themselves and working excessively to the extent that it becomes damaging to their health, then the perfectionist belief is clearly detrimental to their well-being, if not their academic grades. Similarly, if generic plans to work hard in exam preparation form safety behaviours, and the student does indeed achieve top grades in all subjects, then perfectionist beliefs are likely to persist which may result in difficulties in other areas of one's life or continue as a risk for anxiety into adulthood.

EXECUTIVE PROCESSING

Based on the appraisal of the forthcoming exam and generic plans for action, the student will formulate a more detailed and comprehensive situationally specific plan for how to go about coping with the forthcoming exam. This can be quite mentally demanding for some persons as they balance competing needs, wishes, and motivations. For instance, a student might be motivated to achieve certain grades in order to fulfil educational or occupational aspiration, and draw on a prototypical plan of action to study hard and prepare thoroughly for the forthcoming exam. At the same that student may also worry about letting themselves and their parents down, added to which they may not be very confident in their ability for that subject. In that case, the possibility of failure, and the consequences of negative self-worth judgements, could activate plans that are equally as important to the student themselves, but that distract from exam preparation. For instance, the person may end up thinking about alternative possibilities for the future if they do not achieve their target grade and how to deal with disappointing oneself and one's parents.

As I described in the first part of this chapter, metacognition plays a central role in executive processes in the S-REF model. The type of metacognition that is referred to in the model is the metacognitive beliefs about worry along with strategies used to monitor and control anxiety that follow from such beliefs. Positive metacognitive beliefs are the view that worry or rumination is helpful in responding to the situation and negative metacognitive beliefs are the view that worry is uncontrollable or dangerous. Examples of positive and negative metacognitive beliefs described by Wells (2009) are shown in the box below.

EXAMPLES OF POSITIVE AND NEGATIVE METACOGNITIVE BELIEFS ABOUT WORRY

Positive Metacognitive Beliefs

- *I need to worry so that I feel better*
- *Worrying or ruminating helps me cope*
- *Worrying helps me get things done*
- *Rumination helps me understand*
- *Something bad would happen if I didn't worry*
- *Analysing my problems will help me find answers*
- *It is important to control my thoughts*
- *Keeping alert to possible threats helps to keep me safe*

Negative Metacognitive Beliefs about Uncontrollability

- *I cannot control my thoughts*
- *If I don't control my worry, it will control me*
- *I can't control my attention*

> Negative Metacognitive Beliefs about Danger and Importance
> - *Worrying too much can harm me*
> - *Some thoughts could make me lose my mind*
> - *Strong emotions are dangerous*
> - *Bad thoughts have the power to make me do bad things*
> - *Some thoughts can make bad things happen*
> - *Thinking something makes it true*
>
> (*Source Wells, 2009*)

If a person does not hold strong positive or negative metacognitive beliefs about worry, they may be able to form an adaptive plan for coping with their forthcoming exam, even if accessing conflicting plans (e.g., wishing to pass vs. worry about letting oneself down) or negative competence beliefs (e.g., "I am no good at science"). In this circumstance, the period of executive processing may be relatively brief and resolved once the plan is formed. However, it is not difficult to see how positive and negative metacognitive beliefs would influence how a student went about dealing with the pressures associated with an important exam.

Positive metacognitive beliefs would lead to increased worry and rumination, being vigilant for signs of situational threat (e.g., a teacher, parent or friend, emphasising the importance of not failing), overthinking and/or overanalysing the situation. In addition to increased worry and rumination (and threat-monitoring in the case of negative danger beliefs), negative metacognitive beliefs would result in trying to suppress one's thoughts or distract oneself. Such monitoring and control strategies leave the person feeling tired and tense, experiencing stress, and result in elevated anxiety, including anxiety disorders. The continued engagement with worry and a focus on one's internal state keeps the cycle of executive processes from switching off and, over time, can become a habitual way of thinking and responding to exam threat situations and become incorporated into the genetic plans for action.

Executive processes also influence how a person interacts with the situation. As already mentioned, one way is that the person is more aware of situations in which they are being evaluated, and this is one way that executive processes exert an influence on the way situational information is handled at an automatic level by the stimulus-driven process network. In addition, the student may engage in maladaptive avoidance or safety behaviours. Avoidance behaviours are a form of coping with feelings of anxiety by avoiding situations in which they are triggered. While school or exam refusal is relatively rare in compulsory educational contexts there are other more subtle ways in which avoidance behaviours can manifest.

These include procrastination (e.g., avoiding starting exam preparation), activities designed to sabotage one's success (e.g., staying up late before an exam playing computer games), and a 'strategic' withdrawal of effort (i.e., avoiding making an effort in lessons or examination preparation). The latter type of avoidance was described as 'strategic' by Marty Covington (2009) when it is used as a way of deflecting negative self-judgements about one's competence by creating a ready-made reason (i.e., "The reason why I did not pass was because I made no effort"). These types of avoidance behaviours are counterproductive as they increase the likelihood of failure and reduce opportunities to develop the acquisition of skills to cope with the situation more effectively, further contributing to ongoing worry. I do not wish to imply that *all* forms of educational disengagement, or lack of engagement, result from exam anxiety but it is something that needs to be considered when it coincides with other indicators of high exam anxiety.

Safety behaviours are similar in that they are forms of coping used to reduce feelings of anxiety by avoiding the feared outcome (e.g., failure and its negative consequences). It is possible that, depending on the specific combination of self-knowledge and metacognitive beliefs, some safety behaviours may result in a student working so hard for an exam that it becomes detrimental to their health or other areas of their life. If we consider the example of a student who might hold positive competence beliefs (e.g., "I am good at science"), but also holds aspirations to study for a competitive university course that requires the highest grades in all subjects (e.g., medicine) combined with family pressure to be a high achiever. If such a student also held strong positive or negative metacognitive beliefs about worry, then concerns about letting themselves and their family down might be amplified and trigger an ongoing episode of executive processing characterised by a cycle of worry, rumination, and self-focused monitoring of one's internal state and situational threat. The positive competence beliefs, however, might result in this student coping by expending all of their effort and time on exam preparation in order to minimise the risk of failure.

This could be seen as an adaptive approach; the student avoids failure, gains a place in their university course, and eventually becomes a successful medic. In the short-term, this strategy might even be adaptive if the executive processes are terminated once exam grades have been received; worry over failure was fuelling achievement. There are, however, risks associated with this type of safety behaviour. The cognitive load is likely to be exhausting and run the risk of 'burnout' (i.e., feeling overwhelmed, cynical, and trapped). Burnout is associated with physical health problems, and additionally, the student may neglect their health (e.g., not eating properly and or exercising), and other elements of their life, such as social relationships. The success of the safety behaviour reinforces them, making it likely that such a strategy would be employed the next time worry-based executive processing was triggered. Thus, the next time this student faces important exams or other forms of high-stakes assessment (common on competitive and academically demanding courses), the same type of executive processing would trigger another period of worry, rumination, and safety behaviours. If such cycles become automated, there is an increased risk of severe distress and chronic anxiety characterised by anxiety disorders. Over time, therefore, it may become apparent that such safety behaviours may be detrimental.

The apparent short-term success of avoidance and safety behaviours in reducing anxiety and/or avoiding the threat also feeds back to self-knowledge. This could be in the form of dysfunctional generic plans for coping (e.g., rumination and avoidance behaviours are effective ways of managing anxiety) and self-beliefs (e.g., a reinforced belief that one is poor at exams following failure). The outcome of executive processes that follow a pattern of CAS thinking and coping is increased state anxiety (i.e., the level of anxiety experienced at any one point), distress, and the associated cognitive interference that negatively impacts achievement. You might recall from Chapter 1 that exam anxiety can be distinguished as a trait (i.e., the general tendency to become anxious in exams) as well as a state (i.e., specific episodes of anxiety). From the perspective of the S-REF model, high levels of trait exam anxiety would arise when a student habitually utilised coping strategies, prompted by metacognitive beliefs, that resulted in ongoing cycles of self-focused worry and rumination about exam failure and its negative consequences. Without intervention to modify or change the processes outlined in the S-REF model, the person remains locked in such cycles. Examination situations continue to be judged as threatening and continue to trigger ongoing cycles of executive processing characterised by the CAS which maintain the anxiety.

In this section, I have provided an explanation, based on the Zeidner and Matthews (2005) extension of the S-REF model, of the central processes that might lead a student to become, and stay, highly exam-anxious. In doing so, I have provided some examples of the type of self-beliefs and forms of coping that are not adaptive in that they result in, or maintain ongoing worry and rumination. While it is not possible to cover every type of belief and coping strategy, my hope is that by explaining the central processes involved in the S-REF, the reader will be able to identify the various ways in which appraisals, self-knowledge, metacognition, and coping processes combine to influence the level of exam anxiety. In the final section of this chapter, we will turn attention to the evidence for the S-REF model.

EVIDENCE FOR THE S-REF MODEL AS AN EXPLANATION OF EXAM ANXIETY

Some of the processes outlined in the S-REF are very well evidenced, others less so. This tends to be, in part, as some processes outlined in the S-REF overlap with other theories of exam anxiety and hence tend to attract more attention from researchers. One of the most well-established links is between exam anxiety and self-knowledge. Persons who have lower competence beliefs typically report higher levels of exam anxiety. Competence beliefs are typically defined and measured as subject-specific academic self-concept or self-efficacy. Although highly related (see Marsh et al., 2019), the former refers to one's perception of competence more generally in a subject (i.e., how have I found learning in the past; how am I compared to others; how will I find learning in the future?), whereas the latter is more focused on whether one expects to succeed in a more specific context (i.e., a lesson activity, a specific piece of work, or an academic subject).

In the meta-analysis conducted by Davina Robson and colleagues (2023), of students aged 5–13 years, a negative correlation of $r = -.39$ was shown between exam anxiety and academic self-efficacy (6,838 participants) and a negative correlation of $r = -.41$ between exam anxiety and academic self-concept (7,449 participants). In another meta-analysis by Nathaniel von der Embse and colleagues (2019) of students in all stages of education (primary school through to graduate education), academic self-efficacy negatively correlated ($r = -.31$) with exam anxiety (9,162 participants). These studies show that exam anxiety is higher when students' confidence in their academic competence, or expectancy to succeed, is lower.

Other academic competence self-beliefs have been less widely studied. However, two of the studies I have been involved in have examined the link between exam anxiety and confidence in one's ability to perform well in exam conditions (i.e., perceived test competence). The first study (Putwain et al., 2010) showed negative correlations between perceived test competence and the different cognitive and affective-physiological components of exam anxiety ($rs = -.21$ to $-.55$) in Year 12 students aged 16–17 years. The second study (Putwain & Aveyard, 2018), which only included the worry component of test anxiety, showed a negative correlation with test competence ($r = -.66$) in Year 11 students aged 15–16 years. When a student is not confident that they can demonstrate their knowledge, skills, and understanding, under exam conditions, their exam anxiety is higher.

Other forms of self-beliefs have also been linked to exam anxiety. One of the most consistent links has been found between exam anxiety and perfectionism. In a meta-analysis of 4,521 participants at all stages of education (primary through to graduate) perfectionist concerns (i.e., a pre-occupation with avoiding errors and making mistakes) showed a positive correlation with exam anxiety ($r = .42$). Other self-beliefs that represent biased or distorted core views of the self (e.g., personalising; "I will not pass this exam because I am a failure"), others (e.g., mind-reading; "my parents will think I am a failure"), and the future (e.g., catastrophising; "If I will fail this exam my whole life will be a failure") have been shown to positively correlated with exam anxiety. For instance, Putwain et al. (2010), showed positive correlations ($rs = .32$ to $.56$) between cognitive biases and the various components of exam anxiety.

Generic plans for action have not been studied specifically. However, links between motivation, which may inform generic plans, have been studied in the form of achievement goals. Broadly speaking, achievement goals are the endpoint a student is trying to achieve in relation to competence judgements (Senko & Tropiano, 2016). Two types of goals that are of particular relevance to exam anxiety are grounded in a fear of failure. A performance-avoidance goal is when a student's aim is to avoid performing lower than others (i.e., peers, classmates, and family members). A mastery-avoidance goal is when a student's aim is to avoid performing worse than they have done in the past or avoid a fail grade or mark (which could be subjectively determined or an official pass/fail). In Robson et al.'s (2023) meta-analysis (4,585 participants), performance-avoidance goals positively correlated with exam anxiety ($r = .17$). In von der Emsbe et al.'s (2018) meta-analysis, exam anxiety positively correlated with performance avoidance goals ($r = .32$) in 3,986 participants and mastery-avoidance goals ($r = .29$) in 1,341 participants. When students' goals are grounded in avoiding failure, their exam anxiety is higher.

The key executive processes in the S-REF model are the appraisal of the forthcoming examination, metacognition, and choice of coping strategies. Several studies have demonstrated that the appraisal of forthcoming exams as important (i.e., they are high-stakes for the student) interacts with competence beliefs (as outlined above, an important self-belief). In a study of 1,953 6th- and 7th-grade secondary school students from the United States, Selkrik et al. (2011) showed exam anxiety was highest when students appraised English and mathematics tests as important, *and* they did not expect to pass. A similar finding was found by Song and Chang (2021) in a sample of 6,908 7th-grade Korean students (aged 14–16 years). Exam anxiety was highest when exams were appraised as valuable, *and* expectancy of success was low. Studies of this type, although rare, are important for demonstrating how different elements of the S-REF combine.

The role of metacognitive beliefs in linking to test anxiety has also been confirmed in research studies. In a sample of undergraduate students (aged 18–62 years), Marcantonio Spada and colleagues (2006) reported positive correlations between test anxiety and positive metacognitive beliefs ($r = .25$), negative metacognitive beliefs ($r = .64$), the need to control thoughts ($r = .39$), and self-monitoring ($r = .25$). Similar findings have been reported in other studies of undergraduate students (Huntley et al., 2022) and in relation to the state anxiety reported 30 minutes prior to an Objective Structured Clinical Examinations sat by undergraduate medical students (Huntley et al., 2023).

Coping is defined and measured in research using specific coping strategies or by grouping similar types of strategies together. It is also worth highlighting a difference in the way that the term *coping* is used in research from its use in everyday life. In everyday life, we might say someone is 'coping' to mean that they are dealing well with some kind of challenge or adversity and 'not coping' to indicate that they are not dealing well. In research, the term 'coping' is used to refer to the strategy (or group of strategies) used. If a person was not dealing well with a challenge or adversity, we would not say in research parlance that they were 'not coping', as strictly speaking some kind of strategy would have been used. Rather, the person would be described as using an unhelpful, ineffective, or maladaptive coping strategy.

A common approach to grouping coping strategies together that was first introduced by Charles Carver and colleagues in 1989 is to distinguish between problem-focused and emotion-focused strategies. Problem-focused strategies are broadly aimed at doing something to address the event or situation causing the threat. These types of strategies include problem-solving (i.e., thinking about the best solution), formulating a plan to deal with the threat, seeking instrumental support (i.e., people who can provide advice or assistance), and suppressing competing activities (e.g., reducing time spent on leisure activities). Emotion-focused strategies are focused on minimising feelings of distress that arise from threat-eliciting events or situations. These types of strategies include seeking emotional social support (i.e., persons to discuss feelings with), reappraising the event or situation to reduce the threat (e.g., reducing the value attached to academic credentials), and acceptance. A third group of coping strategies, proposed by James Parker and Norman Endler (1992), are related to avoidance. Avoidance strategies include suppressing thoughts and feelings or distracting oneself. Comprehensive reviews (Skinner & Zimmer-Gembeck, 2007; Zeidner, 1995) have concluded that problem-focused strategies are generally considered to be the most adaptive long-term approaches. In contrast, emotion-focused strategies can provide immediate relief from emotional distress but are less effective than long-term strategies since they do not resolve the cause of the threat. Avoidance strategies, however, like those described in the context of the S-REF model are ineffective in that they do not address the threat or the emotion. Of course, a student may use combinations of problem-focused, emotion-focused, and avoidance approaches, although at times, they may come into conflict, and one approach is likely to dominate.

Studies have shown that exam anxiety positively correlates with emotion-focused and avoidance strategies (Matthews et al., 1999; Zeidner, 1994, 1996). Consistent with the S-REF model, highly exam-anxious students respond by trying to avoid or control feelings of anxiety. In contrast, the aforementioned studies showed inconsistent relations between exam anxiety and problem-focused strategies (sometimes positively correlated and sometimes negatively correlated). The inconsistency may be partly due to the use of groups of problem-focused coping strategies, not all of which may be relevant to dealing with exam pressures. An alternative approach I have employed is to specifically focus on the coping strategies most commonly used during exam preparation. According to Joachim Stöber (2004), these are task orientation and preparation (i.e., focusing on exam preparation and temporarily putting other activities to one side; a specific problem-focused strategy), seeking social support (i.e., a mix of emotional and instrumental support), and avoidance (i.e., avoiding thinking about the exam or exam preparation).

In one study conducted by myself and colleagues with students in Years 10 and 11 (aged 14–16 years) preparing for the GCSEs (Putwain et al., 2012), exam anxiety negatively correlated with task-focus and preparation ($rs = -.14$ to $-.48$ for the different components of exam anxiety) and, positively correlated with avoidance ($rs = .14$ to $.30$ for the different components of exam anxiety, excluding test irrelevant thinking). Seeking social support was unrelated to exam anxiety, with the exception of test-irrelevant thinking that showed a negative correlation ($r = -.30$). In summary, findings from studies into the relations between exam anxiety and coping show that, in the main, highly exam-anxious persons deal with exam pressures by using strategies designed to control or avoid anxiety rather than focusing on exam preparation.

Several studies have examined how exam anxiety can relate to maladaptive situational interactions, as proposed in the S-REF model. One type of study uses computerised tasks (see Figure 5.2) to ascertain where persons are focusing their attention. One type of task, referred to as a dot-probe task, briefly presents two stimuli (typically for half a second) that differ in their threat level (e.g., threat vs. neutral) on different parts of the computer screen (e.g., the top and bottom). These stimuli could be words (e.g., exam vs. chair) or pictures (e.g., a picture of an exam setting vs. a picture of a chair). They are replaced with an arrow pointing to the left or to the right, usually also for half a second. The arrow replaces the threat stimuli in 50% of cases and neutral stimuli in the other 50% of cases.

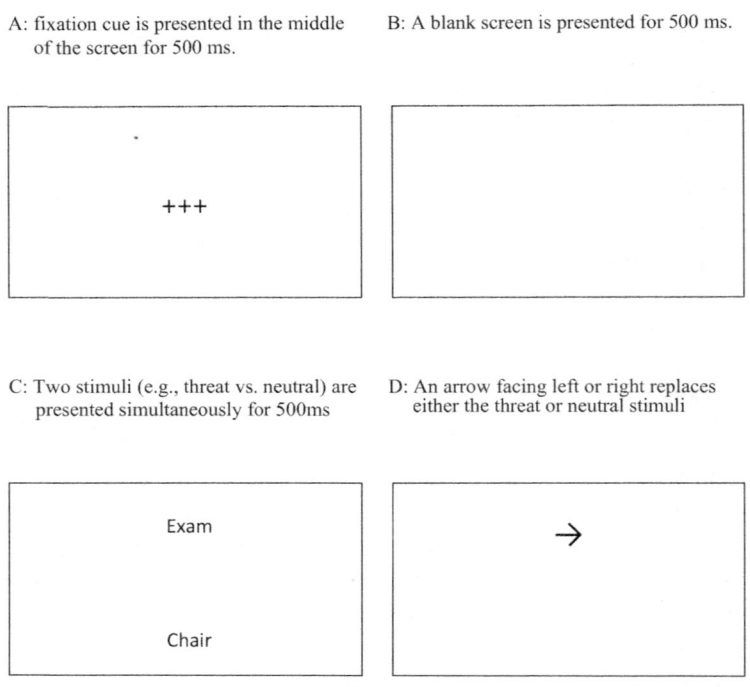

Figure 5.2 The Presentation of Stimuli in a Dot-Probe Task.

The person tries to respond as quickly and accurately as possible by pressing one key on a keyboard for the left arrow and another key on the right (e.g., the letters Z and M on a standard QWERTY English language keyword).

The reaction times for responding to the arrows replacing the threat and neutral words are then compared. The rationale is that if anxious persons are vigilant for threat cues in the environment, their attention will be more quickly drawn to the threat stimuli. They will, therefore, show quicker responses to the arrows replacing threat stimuli than neutral stimuli. In contrast, non-anxious persons will not be more likely to focus attention on the threat than the neutral stimuli and they would not be any quicker at responding to one type of stimuli than the other.

Reviews of numerous studies have shown that highly anxious students respond more quickly to threat, than non-threat stimuli (Van Bockstaele et al., 2014). This phenomenon is referred to as attention bias. Fewer studies have specifically studied attention bias in relation to exam anxiety. In one dot-probe study I conducted with colleagues (Putwain et al., 2011), highly exam-anxious undergraduate students in an evaluative-situation responded more quickly to arrows replacing threat words than neutral words (i.e., showed an attention bias towards threat).

Another study of undergraduate students by Jastrowski Mano and colleagues (2018), used picture stimuli (exam threat vs. neutral) rather than words, and also found an attention bias towards threat in highly exam-anxious participants, which was more pronounced in female participants. An alternative approach to the dot-probe task is to ask participants to wear glasses that track eye-gaze and hence provide an indicator of where visual attention is directed. In one study of this type, Cenlow Hou and colleagues (2023) used a visual search task. Participants were shown a target picture (exam threat vs. neutral) and then had to identify whether that picture was included in a group of four pictures presented together (a visual search task) as accurately and quickly as possible. Highly exam-anxious participants focused their visual attention more quickly on the test-threat pictures when presented alongside other non-threat pictures indicating an attention bias towards threat. The dot-probe and eye-tracking studies confirm that, like other forms of anxiety, exam-anxious individuals are alert to signs of exam-related threats in their environment.

In addition to attention bias, numerous studies have shown that academic self-handicapping and procrastination are linked to greater exam anxiety. For instance, a meta-analysis of 35 studies, comprising 36,581 participants in all stages of education (primary school through to undergraduate), showed a positive correlation of $r = .29$ between self-handicapping and exam anxiety (Schwinger et al., 2022). With respect to procrastination, a review of six studies showed positive correlations ($rs = .20$ to $.45$) with exam anxiety (Preiss et al., 2006). These studies confirm that, as predicted in the S-REF, maladaptive person-situation interactions, like safety- and avoidance-behaviours, are associated with greater exam anxiety.

The studies I have described in the final section of this analysis provide evidence for the various processes outlined in the S-REF model. However, they do so in a rather piecemeal fashion. For instance, evidencing the links between self-beliefs and exam anxiety separately from executive processes and behaviours. Few studies have attempted more comprehensive evaluations of the S-REF model that bring together different processes. In one such study (Putwain, 2019), I asked Year 11 students preparing for GCSE exams to report one key self-belief, two key executive processes related to coping, and one key maladaptive behaviour, along with the cognitive (worry) component of exam anxiety. The self-belief was academic control, namely the extent to which students believe they can exert control over success and failure through their academic competence, effort, and study strategy. The executive processes were cognitive reappraisal (i.e., re-evaluating a situation to reduce its emotional impact) and expressive suppression (i.e., the inhibition of emotional behaviour). The maladaptive behaviour was self-handicapping (i.e., avoiding examination preparation).

Results showed that when combined into a single analytic model, students with stronger academic control beliefs reported fewer exam worries. Students who used more cognitive reappraisal, however, reported greater exam worry. In turn, higher worry was related to subsequent lower GCSE grades, and greater use of academic self-handicapping predicted lower academic control beliefs. These various links provide support for the S-REF model. Positive self-beliefs (like higher control) are associated with reduced exam worry and maladaptive avoidance-based interactions with the situation, like academic self-handicapping, reinforce the belief that one has little control over academic success and failure. Coping strategies like cognitive reappraisal are used more frequently when exam worries are greater. Over time, it might be expected for this strategy to reduce exam worries, and anxiety more generally, but as already mentioned, this may come at a cost.

A second study to bring together different processes involved in the S-REF model was conducted by Jerrell Cassady and colleagues (2024). They considered intolerance of uncertainty, a self-belief not widely studied in relation to test anxiety, alongside self-handicapping behaviours, and aggregated grades, in a sample of undergraduate students from the United States. Intolerance of uncertainty is when the lack of predictability in a situation (e.g., not knowing which questions might appear on an exam, or exam grades being uncertain) is threatening or unbearable. Results showed intolerance of uncertainty was strongly linked to greater exam anxiety. Greater exam anxiety was, in turn, linked to greater use of self-handicapping, and lower grades. More studies of this type are needed that incorporate the different processes involved in the S-REF model to examine how they operate in tandem.

CHAPTER SUMMARY

In this chapter, I have outlined the S-REF model of anxiety, how this model can be applied to exam anxieties specifically, and the evidence for this model. The various processes proposed in the S-REF are, in the main, well-evidenced in a somewhat fragmented fashion. While theoretical explanations of psychological processes can only ever be simplified versions of people's actual experiences, we can be reasonably confident, nonetheless, that the S-REF model provides an accurate account of how and why some persons become more exam-anxious than others. One of the advantages of having a detailed and well-evidenced account of the processes that lead to greater exam anxiety is that it offers possibilities for how interventions can be designed to disrupt these very processes, lead to a more effective management of exam pressures, and ultimately to lower exam anxiety. In the next chapter, we will turn attention to this topic and consider what types of intervention could effectively lower exam anxiety and the evidence for them.

6

INTERVENTIONS FOR EXAM ANXIETY
WHAT CAN BE DONE ABOUT IT

SETTING THE SCENE

Many schools, colleges, and universities in the UK, and elsewhere, are taking action to support the well-being and mental health of their students, including dealing with the pressures of taking exams. I have seen a variety of approaches implemented in schools to support the well-being of their students, including, but not limited to, yoga, mindfulness (i.e., focusing attention on the 'here and now'), and pet therapy (i.e., stroking sociable animals). It strikes me that the offer of these types of activities is largely driven by the local knowledge of what might work by the person responsible for supporting student well-being balanced against the availability and cost of implementing them. I have no doubt that yoga and mindfulness can provide a temporary break from the pressures of life, including those of exams, and that interacting with sociable animals can be greatly enjoyable for pet lovers. In that sense, based on anecdotal evidence, they do seem to provide a temporary boost for well-being and that is a good thing. However, what happens when one returns to face the pressures of school, exams, and so on?

My concern is that these approaches may not bring a long-term benefit unless they also involve a change of one's mindset or outlook about exam pressures (what psychologists would call 'cognitive change') and how to cope with them. In the first two sections of this chapter, I will consider psychological interventions for exam anxiety. By 'psychological interventions', I mean activities designed to assist students in coping with exam pressures, and reduce exam anxiety, based on psychological theory and technique. The advantage of considering psychological interventions is that they are typically subjected to formal and rigorous evaluation to establish their effectiveness in ways that other activities to support students are not always. This allows schools, colleges, and universities, who may have limited resources, to be able to make an informed choice based on an evidence-based intervention (i.e., one with evidence to support its effectiveness).

PSYCHOLOGICAL INTERVENTIONS FOR EXAM ANXIETY

In this section, I will summarise the findings from three meta-analyses and two systematic reviews, which provide evidence of the effectiveness of exam anxiety interventions. I have already cited findings from Ray Hembree's (1988) meta-analysis in Chapter 3 pertaining to the relations between exam anxiety and achievement. Hembree's study also included 137 studies from 1952 to 1986 (7,641 individuals in various stages of education from primary school through to university) of interventions that compared exam anxiety scores pre- and post-intervention, to a control group that did not receive the intervention (or received it at a later point, referred to as a wait-list control group). The advantage of this design is that if we observe a reduction in exam anxiety scores for the group receiving the intervention, we can rule out the possibility that this change would have occurred anyway over time, by comparing their scores to those of the control group. When this design involves a random allocation of persons to the intervention or control-list wait group, it is referred to as a 'randomised control trial' and is considered as the gold standard for evidence of an intervention's effectiveness.

Hembree grouped interventions into those that targeted the affective-physiological component of exam anxiety (referred to as behavioural intervention), those that targeted the cognitive component of exam anxiety (referred to as cognitive intervention), those that targeted both (cognitive-behavioural intervention), and those focused on study or test-taking skills. As different studies included in the meta-analysis used different scales to measure exam anxiety, as is typical for meta-analyses, they were converted to a standardised metric. In Hembree's case, there was an effect size named Glass's Δ. Δs reported in Hembree's study show the difference in exam anxiety for the intervention group, post-intervention, relative to the control group.[1] Behavioural (Δs = −.54 to −1.10), cognitive (Δ = −.34), cognitive-behavioural (Δs = −.53 and −.87), test-taking skills (Δ = −.55), and combined study and test-taking skills (Δ = −.52) interventions were all effective in reducing exam anxiety relative to a group that did not receive an intervention. Furthermore, combined behavioural and study skills (Δ = −1.22) and cognitive-behavioural (Δ = −.83) interventions were also effective in reducing exam anxiety.

Hembree's study is the only meta-analysis of the three to have also considered the effect of exam anxiety intervention on achievement. In 114 studies (6,488 individuals), desensitisation[2] (Δ = .32), cognitive-behavioural (Δ = .52), study skills (Δ = .39), and study skills with desensitisation (Δ = .76) interventions were all effective in boosting test performance relative to a control group. In 45 studies (1,303 individuals), desensitisation (Δ = .40), cognitive-behavioural (Δ = .72), and study skills (Δ = .73) interventions were all effective in boosting Grade Point Average (i.e., average student grades), relative to a control group.

The second meta-analysis, conducted by Tuncay Ergene (2003), included 56 studies from 1974 to 1998 (2,428 individuals aged 10–32 years although the mean age was 19 years and the majority were in university education). Interventions were grouped into similar categories to those used by Hembree, but used a slightly different method of calculating the effect size was used, namely Cohen's d.[3] Behavioural ($d = .80$), cognitive ($d = .63$), cognitive-behavioural ($d = .36$), study and test-taking skills ($d = .42$), cognitive with study and test-taking skills ($d = 1.22$), behavioural with study and test-taking skills ($d = 1.10$), and cognitive-behavioural with study and test-taking skills ($d = .72$) interventions were effective in reducing exam anxiety.

The third meta-analysis was conducted by Chris Huntley and colleagues (2019). This meta-analysis contained 44 studies of interventions used with undergraduate students from 1970 to 2017 (comprising 2,209 individuals). Interventions were grouped into anxiety training (i.e., behavioural methods) and cognitive-behavioural (i.e., cognitive or cognitive-behavioural) approaches, alone or in combination, and assessed the effectiveness of interventions using Hedges' g[3]. Anxiety training ($g = -.83$), cognitive-behavioural ($g = -.58$), and combined anxiety training and cognitive-behavioural ($g = -1.38$) approaches were all effective in reducing exam anxiety. Huntley et al. also analysed data from 12 studies that had included a follow-up wave of data collection after the intervention was completed (this ranged from 3 to 26 weeks, with a mean of 9.4 weeks). Although there was insufficient data to compare all intervention types, relaxation training ($g = -1.12$), and cognitive-behavioural ($g = -.40$), approaches showed reduced exam anxiety for intervention compared to control groups (i.e., that the effect of the intervention remained over time).

The results of these three meta-analyses are extremely encouraging in showing that psychological interventions can be effective in reducing exam anxiety and boosting exam performance and average grades. In addition, many of the categories of intervention showed moderate to large effects. However, understanding which of these interventions are most effective for school-aged students (i.e., those in primary and secondary education under the age of 19 years) is difficult. Huntley's sample comprised solely, and Ergene's sample mainly, of undergraduate students. Hembree's study did include samples of younger students (Grade 5 upwards) but a comparison of interventions for students of different ages, or stages of education, was not possible due to the small number of studies of participants under 18 year or under. Two systematic analyses, however, have reviewed the evidence for interventions designed for, and delivered to, samples of students in primary and secondary school.

The first systematic review identified just ten studies from 2000 to 2010 evaluating exam anxiety interventions for students aged 19 years or under (von der Embse & colleagues, 2013). Interventions included those already included in the above three meta-analyses (desensitisation, study and test-taking skills, relaxation, and cognitive-behavioural) in addition to biofeedback,[4] providing guided-feedback during a low-stakes test, confidence building, guided visualisation, and psychoeducation.[5] All but one study (a cognitive-behavioural intervention) showed reductions for one or more components of exam anxiety following intervention, relative to a control, group.

The second systematic review, conducted by David Soares and Kevin Woods (2020), identified a further 11 studies from 2011 to 2018 for students aged 19 years or under. Ten interventions were designed to reduce exam anxiety and included cognitive-behavioural, relaxation and desensitisation, mindfulness (colouring-in), scheduling a physical education (PE) class prior to a test, cognitive bias modification,[6] thinking about how to solve mathematics problems before taking a test, and using play and performance in group settings to explore feelings about taking tests. With two exceptions (PE and performance) all interventions showed a reduction in exam anxiety compared to a control group. Taking a PE class prior to a test had no effect on exam anxiety and the study examining play/performance did not measure exam anxiety or use a control group, making it difficult to draw a reliable conclusion. Of the remaining studies, those with the strongest methodological quality and which showed the strongest reduction were the more 'traditional' interventions using cognitive-behavioural, and relaxation and desensitisation approaches. The remaining intervention considered different pre-test learning strategies (practice tests, writing summaries, or re-reading) on knowledge retention. For highly exam-anxious students, writing summaries was the most effective strategy, whereas practice tests were the most effective for low exam-anxious students.

These two systematic reviews show how interventions can be used to successfully reduce exam anxiety in school-aged populations. There are a number of different intervention approaches showing strong evidence that could be utilised by primary and secondary schools to support highly exam-anxious students. These include interventions focused on controlling emotional or physiological reactions to exam anxiety (e.g., relaxation, desensitisation, and biofeedback), those focused on controlling anxiety-related beliefs (e.g., cognitive and cognitive-behavioural intervention), and those focused on behaviours (e.g., study and test-taking skills).

COGNITIVE-BEHAVIOURAL INTERVENTION

In this section, I will explore in greater detail how cognitive-behavioural intervention (CBI) can be used to support high exam-anxious secondary school students by considering two specific examples. Of the various interventions that have been shown to be successful, I have chosen to focus on CBI for three reasons. First, a systematic review of all interventions for anxiety (not just exam anxiety) in children and young people from 1970 to 2011 found CBI to be the *only* psychological intervention to meet the criteria for being a well-established and efficacious intervention (Higa-McMillan, et al., 2016). Second, modern CBI frameworks are sufficiently flexible to integrate emotional, cognitive, behavioural, and skills-based approaches. Third, CBI can be designed in ways that are brief and straightforward to implement in school settings.

Modern approaches to CBI are based on the idea shown in Figure 6.1 (Williams & Chellingsworth, 2010). There are two important principles to highlight. First, thoughts, emotions, behaviours, and physiology are all mutually inter-related. That is, how we think will influence our emotions, behaviour, and physiology. Similarly, how we behave will influence our thoughts, emotions, and physiology, and so on. This works in both positive and negative directions.

Biased thoughts, for instance "unless I receive a top grade, I am a failure", could result in emotional arousal (a physiological response), feelings of panic and being overwhelmed (an emotional response), and distracting oneself from starting exam preparation (a behavioural response). Learning to relax, or control one's anxiety (i.e., a physiological intervention) when preparing for and taking exams, could change thinking ("I can cope with exam pressures"), reduce feelings of panic and being overwhelmed, and reduce avoidance behaviours. Second, situations and thoughts are mutually related (i.e., changing thinking can change the perception of the situation, and changing the situation could change how we think).

Next, I would like to explain two CBIs to illustrate how they can be used to reduce exam anxiety based on these principles. The first is Strategies for Tackling Exam Pressure and Stress (STEPS) that I developed with Anthony Daly, Suzanne Chamberlain, and Shireen Sadreddini. STEPS is a manualised, brief, low-intensity CBI comprising six sessions, each lasting approximately 60 mins.[7] Each session has a different focus (see Figure 6.1) and contains a mixture of psychoeducation, reflective activities, practice of intervention techniques, quiz-based reinforcement, and follow-up activities. It is accompanied by a student booklet for students to record their reflective activities and follow-up tasks to practise between sessions.

STEPS follows central CBI principles, like those outlined in Figure 6.1 of modifying thoughts, physiology, and behaviour, in positive ways to reduce anxiety. It is also based on the S-REF model (Zeidner & Matthews, 2005; see Chapter 5) to ensure that the negative self-knowledge, executive processes, and maladaptive behaviours, that enhance and maintain high levels of exam anxiety, are all targeted. Some anxiety interventions based on the S-REF model, which specifically target the CAS (Wells, 2009; see Chapter 5), are referred to as meta-cognitive therapy (MCT). The specific aim of MCT is to identify and challenge the positive and negative metacognitive beliefs about anxiety that result in ineffective coping strategies that maintain anxiety.

Although STEPS targets the central components of the S-REF model, it is not specifically a MCT. Rather, the cognitive elements

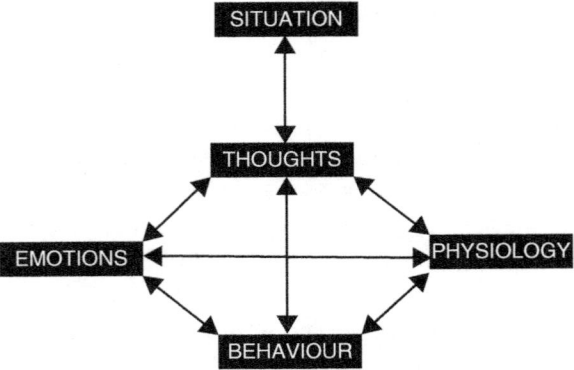

Figure 6.1 The Five Areas of Cognitive-Behavioural Intervention.

of STEPS in Sessions 2 and 5 adopt a more 'classic' CBI approach (see Beck, 1979) which is to identify and challenge biased, unrealistic, and self-defeating thoughts (referred to as automatic negative thoughts). While this does not rule out identifying and challenging metacognitive beliefs per se, it is not the specific focus of STEPS. I would characterise STEPS as a multimodal intervention, one that draws on different CBI traditions in an integrative fashion.

STEPS was originally developed due to the lack of widely available supports available for schools and colleges to use with students aged 14–19 years preparing for, and taking, high-stakes exams (such as GCSEs and A Levels). STEPS was initially trailed as a self-help tool whereby students would work through materials on their own during a designated school lesson or after school in their own time. This approach was delivered as a universal intervention[8] with 3,225 participants aged 14–16 years from ten English secondary schools (Putwain et al., 2014). Participants were randomly allocated to intervention or wait-list groups and measures of the worry and tension components of test anxiety were taken pre- and post-intervention.

Perhaps unsurprisingly, only 13.7% of the intervention group completed STEPS (25.5% partially completed the programme; one or more of the six sessions) and 60.8% chose not to complete any of the programme. When participants were asked to complete STEPS at home, 86.9% did not complete any sessions. While disappointing, these results are still useful in two ways. First, it underlines that STEPS was not appropriate as a universal intervention. The feedback received from participants with low and moderate exam anxiety was that they simply did not see STEPS as useful; it was, in the words of one participant, "not for me". Second, self-help was not an appropriate model of delivery and requires a level of motivation and self-regulation that is beyond the reach of most adolescents aged 14–16 years (and likely beyond). While disappointing, these findings are instructive in pointing to a more effective delivery model. This is a point we shall return to.

THE SIX STEPS SESSIONS

Session	Brief Description
1	• Recognising the signs of stress and anxiety • Understanding the reasons why students find exams stressful • Understanding the effects of stress and anxiety
2	• Understanding how feelings and behaviours are linked to thoughts • Identifying automatic negative thoughts (ANTs) • Challenging ANTs and replacing them with positive self-talk
3	• The physical signs of stress • Deep breathing and muscle relaxation techniques • Reflecting on how these work for you
4	• Learning principles • Learning and revision strategies • Planning revision
5	• Goal setting • Visualisation • Personalising visualisation
6	• Exams Day • Recap of the STEPS sessions • Reflecting on what works best for you

Highly exam-anxious participants who had completed STEPS showed moderate declines in the worry ($d = .63$) and tension ($d = .52$) components of exam anxiety compared to control group participants (see Figure 6.2).[9] Participants who were low or moderately exam-anxious showed no change in worry and tension scores pre- to post-intervention. Although we were not able to make proper use of the original random allocation of participants to intervention and control conditions, as we selected only those participants who had completed STEPS for this analysis, these findings offer encouragement that STEPS had the potential to reduce anxiety. They also further underscore that STEPS is of limited use as a universal intervention; it is of benefit to high exam-anxious participants only.

Subsequently, I moved to a model whereby STEPS was delivered by a trained facilitator to small groups of 6–10 students in face-to-face settings, and specifically offered to students who were highly exam-anxious (i.e., selective intervention). In a study evaluating this model of delivery conducted with Marc Pescod (Putwain & Pescod, 2018), 426 secondary school students, aged 14–16 years, were screened using the

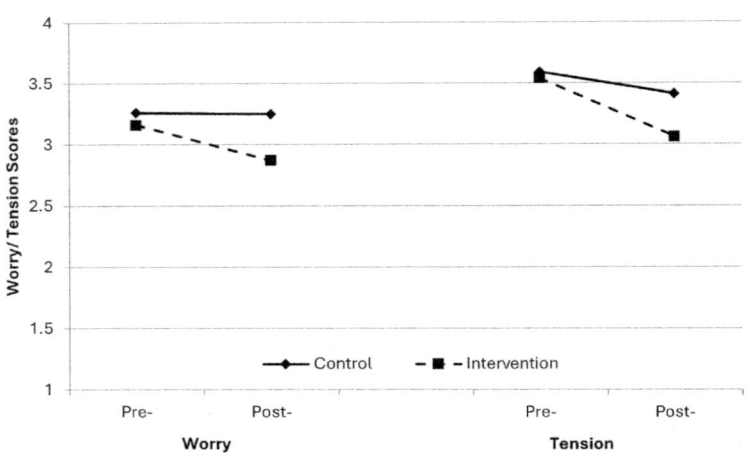

Figure 6.2 Pre- and Post-Intervention Worry and Tension Scores for High Exam-Anxious Intervention and Control Group Participants (Putwain et al., 2014).

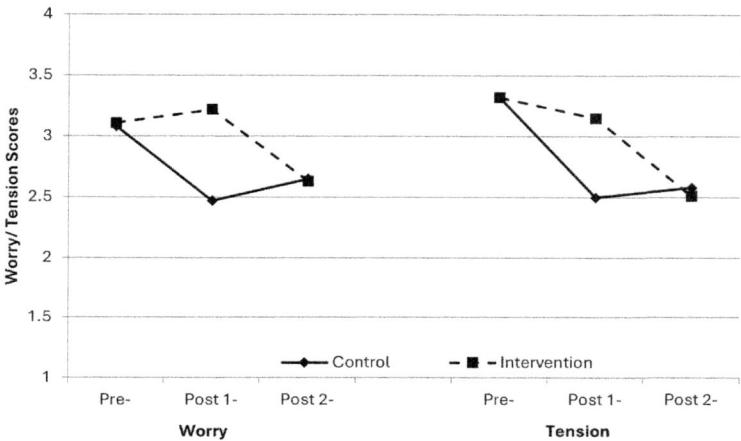

Figure 6.3 Pre- and Post-Intervention Worry and Tension Scores for High Exam-Anxious Intervention and Control Group Participants (Putwain & Pescod, 2018).

Revised Test Anxiety Scale (RTA: Hagtvet & Benson, 1997). Fifty-six students reported scores in the upper 66th scale percentile (i.e., were judged to be highly exam-anxious) and were randomly allocated to intervention (25 students) or wait-list control (31 students) groups. Over the course of the study, five students in each group withdrew their participation. Data were collected after the intervention group had completed STEPS and again after the wait-list control group had completed STEPS.

Participants who had completed STEPS showed a moderate decline in worry ($d = .76$) and a large decline in the tension ($d = 1.14$) components of exam anxiety compared to control group participants (see Figure 6.3). The wait-list control participants also showed similar reductions in worry ($d = .79$) and tension ($d = .80$) components of exam anxiety after they had received the intervention.[10] An additional facet of this study looked at whether uncertain control was a possible mechanism by which STEPS reduced exam anxiety (a *mediating* variable). Uncertain control is when a student does not understand how or why they have achieved (or not achieved) a particular grade or test score. They cannot see a link from their study- or test-taking strategy, or their perceived ability, to grades or test scores. As a result, they are not confident about their likelihood of success in exams and anticipate failure. In the S-REF model, this would be a self-knowledge belief.

Uncertain control showed a moderate decline ($d = .64$) after STEPS was completed by the intervention group, relative to the control group, and again for the wait-list control group ($d = 47$). Put another way, we could say that participants judged themselves to be more in control after completing STEPS. A mediational analysis showed that the reduction in uncertain control underpinned the reduction in worry and tension. These findings show that the facilitated and selective model of delivery was effective in reducing exam anxiety and consistent with the S-REF model. One of the reasons why STEPS was effective was by increasing students' perception of their control over their forthcoming exam performance and grade. An additional finding is that while the worry and tension scores of the intervention group increased slightly over the six-week period while the wait-list control received their intervention, the increase was negligible and not statistically significant.

A third study, conducted with Nathaniel von der Embse (2021), screened 1,073 students aged 14–16 years, identifying 161 highly exam-anxious students (i.e., those in the upper 66th percentile of RTA scale scores) eligible for intervention. Participants were randomly allocated to interventions (80 students) or wait-list control (81 students) groups. Over the course of the study, five students in the intervention, and ten in the wait-list control, groups withdrew their participation. Data were collected before and after the intervention group had completed STEPS. Unfortunately, in this study we were unable to collect data after the wait-list control group had completed STEPS.

In addition to exam anxiety, we also collected pre- and post-intervention scores for school-related well-being, and symptoms of GAD and PD. Highly exam-anxious participants who had completed STEPS showed a large decline in exam anxiety scores

($d = .86$), and moderate declines in GAD ($d = .43$) and PD ($d = .54$) symptoms relative to control group participants. STEPS had no effect on school-related well-being. This is likely a result of exam pressures, and how one deals with them, being just one contributor of many to one's overall level of school-related well-being. In addition, the reduction of GAD and PD symptoms was mediated by the reduction in test anxiety symptoms, which further emphasises the common links between these different aspects of anxiety.

In addition to these formal evaluations of STEPS, I have collected feedback from students at schools who I work in partnership with. I have provided some examples of narrative feedback in the box below from students aged 14–18 years. These first-hand narratives provide powerful and compelling testimony of how students can benefit. Based on student feedback on STEPS and which elements could be improved, I recently developed an updated version (STEPS v2.0) with Christine Roberts, Emma Rainbird, and Tahrim Hussain. The focus of the six sessions remains as before, but we reduced the psychoeducational content and increased the use of group-based activity within the sessions. In addition, I developed a training package for staff in schools and colleges who may not have a background in CBI to be able to learn the core skills required to deliver STEPS (this is described in Putwain et al., 2023). STEPS materials and training are available through the British Psychological Society's online learning platform (BPS Learn).

NARRATIVE FEEDBACK FROM STUDENTS AFTER COMPLETING STEPS

"Before doing STEPS I was extremely worried about doing my GCSEs as my mocks stressed me out. After doing STEPS I feel confidence as I know I will concentrate when doing breathing exercises. The skills I have learnt are visualisation, deep breathing, muscle relaxation, and revision timetables. Before STEPS I was not confident in myself and let my struggles during mocks get the best of me.

> *Now I feel like I can go into an exam and feel stress-free as I can only do my best".*
>
> *"Before doing STEPS I had no idea how to handle my mind going blank or freezing during exams. Now I am quite confident that I could employ techniques such as deep breathing and visualisation in order to help me continue and power through my exam. The segment about revision techniques has made me realise some useful alternate ways to revise that better suit my way of learning. I feel much more comfortable with preparing and sitting my A-Level exams now".*
>
> *"Before STEPS I had been in CBT therapy before, so a lot of stuff wasn't new to me, but I think it definitely still helped having someone there going through stuff with you and reminding you of things you had forgotten. Skills I developed are addressing automatic negative thoughts, visualisation, having a relaxing thing before an exam".*
>
> *"Before STEPS I thought I wouldn't be able to pass my GCSEs and was having a lot of stress. I am a lot more confident and prepared now as I know how to calm my nerves. The skills I learnt were how to control my breathing and muscle relaxation. I feel a lot less anxious now and have changed the way I feel about exams in general".*

The second CBI I would like to briefly consider is called the Pastel programme, developed by Gabrielle Yale-Soulière and colleagues in Canada and intended for use with adolescent students in secondary or upper secondary education. The Pastel programme comprises six one-hour workshops that include elements of education on test anxiety, cognitive restructuring (i.e., identifying and challenging biased and unhelpful beliefs, avoidance and exposure, relaxation, study strategies and problem-solving; see *The Six Pastel Sessions*). Pastel sessions were delivered in small groups of up to 12 students by a professional with training in CBT (e.g., school counsellor, social worker, or practitioner psychologist).

THE SIX PASTEL SESSIONS

Session	Brief Description
1	• Understating test anxiety: triggers, sensations, and consequences
2	• Understanding avoidance and exposure, challenging unhelpful thoughts, organising a realistic study schedule
3	• Graduated exposure to challenges and understanding perfectionism, continuing with realistic study schedules
4	• Continuing graduated exposure challenges and realistic study schedules, understanding problem solving strategies
5	• Continuing graduated exposure challenges, realistic study schedules, and problem-solving strategies
6	• Consolidate knowledge and plan for future triggers for test anxiety

In a randomised control trial to evaluate the effectiveness of the Pastel programme, Yale-Soulière and colleagues (2024) screened 385 students aged 14–17 years from five Canadian secondary schools using the Friedben Test Anxiety Scale. Forty-eight highly exam-anxious students (those scoring at the 58th scale percentile) were randomly allocated to intervention or control conditions (24 in each). Over the course of the study, one student from each group withdrew their participation. Participants who had completed the Pastel programme showed moderate reductions in post-intervention test anxiety ($d = .56$) and social anxiety ($d = .54$), and smaller reductions in test anxiety ($d = .37$) and social anxiety ($d = .22$) at a six-month follow-up.

HOW CAN SCHOOLS AND COLLEGES SUPPORT HIGHLY EXAM-ANXIOUS STUDENTS?

Besides interventions, there are other strategies schools and colleges can use to support highly exam-anxious studies, although remarkably few studies have researched this question.[11] However, we can take findings from participants who are students in schools or colleges and consider how they can be usefully applied on a wider scale. I do not wish to suggest these are 'one size fits all' approaches. Some approaches will be more suitable for older students, and there will be various local issues (e.g., school timetabling, student cohorts, and so on) which may make approaches more suitable for one school or college than another).

TAKING EXAMS UNDER STANDARDISED CONDITIONS

Perhaps one of the most straightforward recommendations, and one that many secondary schools and colleges will be doing already, is to normalise the experience of taking exams under standardised conditions. This can help to reduce additional pressures on students associated with the ritual and theatre of standardised conditions (e.g., silence, seated in rows in a large room such as a sports hall, with an unknown invigilator, and so on). The meta-analyses I briefly reviewed above showed desensitisation was an effective strategy to reduce exam anxiety. In addition, a study of undergraduates has specifically shown a reduction in exam anxiety in students tested every week for ten weeks compared to those only given a final exam (Zimmer & Hocevar, 1994).

The implication is that the more students experience taking exams under standardised settings, the less unusual these settings will be. Therefore, students should not be left to experience taking exams under standardised settings for the first time when those exams are high stakes (e.g., GCSE exams in Year 11, or mock GCSE exams in Year 10 or 11). Rather, students should be exposed to taking exams under standardised settings in secondary school regularly (i.e., at least once per year) and as early as possible (i.e., from the first year of secondary school onwards) when the stakes of exams are lower. Where it is not logistically possible to schedule exams in large school halls, the classroom setting will still provide some experience of the standardised exam experience.

TEST-TAKING SKILLS

Reducing additional pressures associated with taking exams is no bad thing, but it will not change the self-knowledge and executive processes that may be contributing to elevated exam anxiety in the first place. The meta-analyses I reviewed also showed that study- and test-taking skills can reduce exam anxiety. Developing these skills will help to build students' confidence and belief that they can exercise a greater degree of control over their exam scores or grades, and both are fundamental in lowering exam anxiety.

In terms of test-taking skills while there are some broad generic skills, a subject-specific approach is likely to be more effective as exam questions and formats, as well as the skills and type of knowledge assessed, vary so widely from one subject to another. As part of exam preparation, students should be given as much information in advance as possible. This includes which curriculum/specification areas are to be examined, time limits, mode or administration, and question and test format. Again, something that many schools and colleges will be doing already is showing students examples of specific exam questions and how marks will be awarded by examiners. In short, it teaches students to think about writing their exam answers from the perspective of what an examiner is looking for, thereby enabling self-assessment.

On the one hand, this is a highly instrumental approach ('teaching to the test') and not in keeping with broader aims of education to nurture and support and develop students' interests, talents, and critical thinking (educere) or develop a workforce for the future. On the other hand, this approach will help to build student's understanding and reduce uncertainty about how they can gain marks for different types of exam questions. As you might recall from the STEPS evaluation study I described above, reducing uncertainty also reduces exam anxiety (Putwain & Pescod, 2018). Students will feel more confident and in control of how to gain marks which will, in turn, lower their exam anxiety.

STUDY SKILLS AND SELF-REGULATED LEARNING

In terms of exam study-skills, or *revision* as it tends to be called in the UK, students, in my experience are often very good at planning and engaging in exam preparation. They will produce detailed, colourful, and ornate, revision timetables and expend effort in engaging with their revision. However, they are less knowledgeable about whether the strategies they use are effective or not. In a similar way to how I have described test-taking skills, not knowing whether a particular strategy is effective or not will create uncertainty and reduce confidence and control. What can be done?

Like test-taking skills, revision strategies are best considered from a subject-specific approach. Some subjects lend themselves more to some revision strategies than others. Within the strategies that are appropriate for a specific subject, students may have a preference for one strategy or find it works more effectively for them than another.[12] Within the approaches that are appropriate for a specific subject, I would recommend that students are exposed to as wide a range of strategies as possible and establish which strategies are most effective for them in low-stakes settings. Examples of different types of revision strategies are shown in Figures 6.4–6.6 (British Psychological Society, 2023).

Some students may be able to try these strategies and work out their effectiveness on their own in self-directed activity. Many students, however, will require such activity to be routinely scheduled into cycles of classroom learning and assessment. These activities should be scheduled well in advance of actual preparation for high-stakes exams. Allowing students to experiment with different strategies and providing feedback from low-stakes tests based on different strategies will help students choose strategies with greater confidence and control so that they can be effective. This will again help to reduce exam anxiety.

INTERVENTIONS FOR EXAM ANXIETY 129

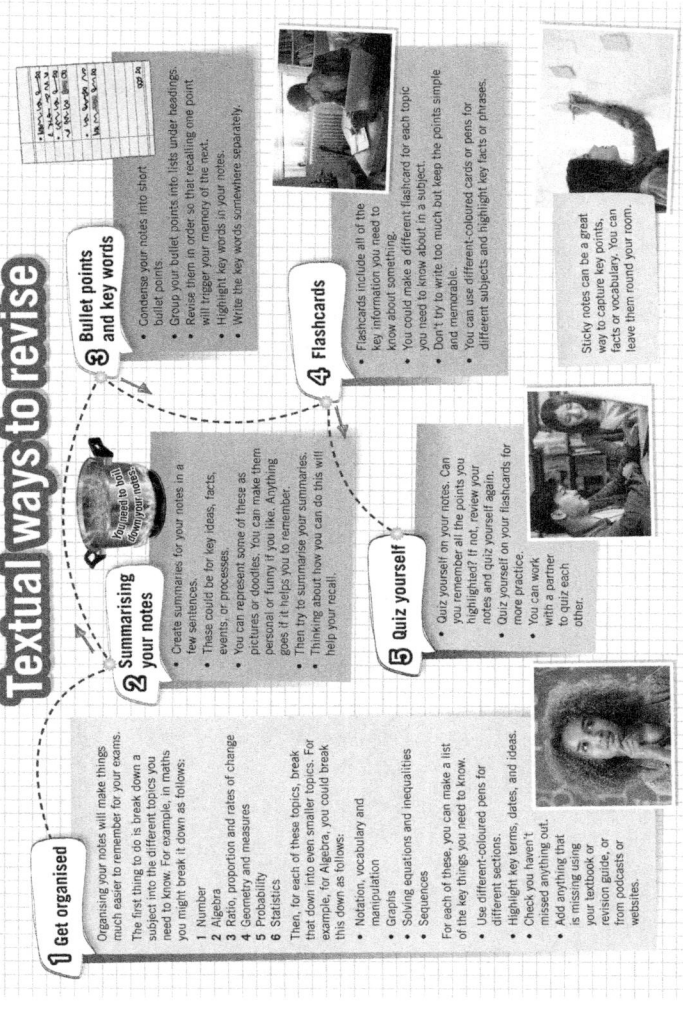

Figure 6.4 Textual Ways to Revise.

130 INTERVENTIONS FOR EXAM ANXIETY

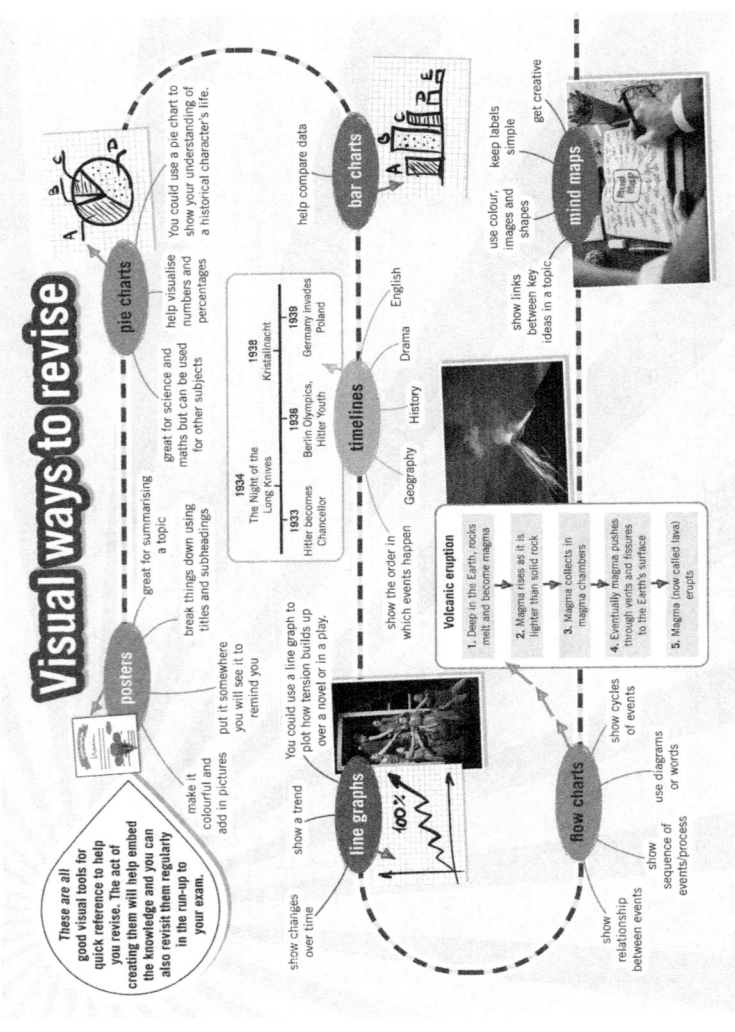

Figure 6.5 Visual Ways to Revise.

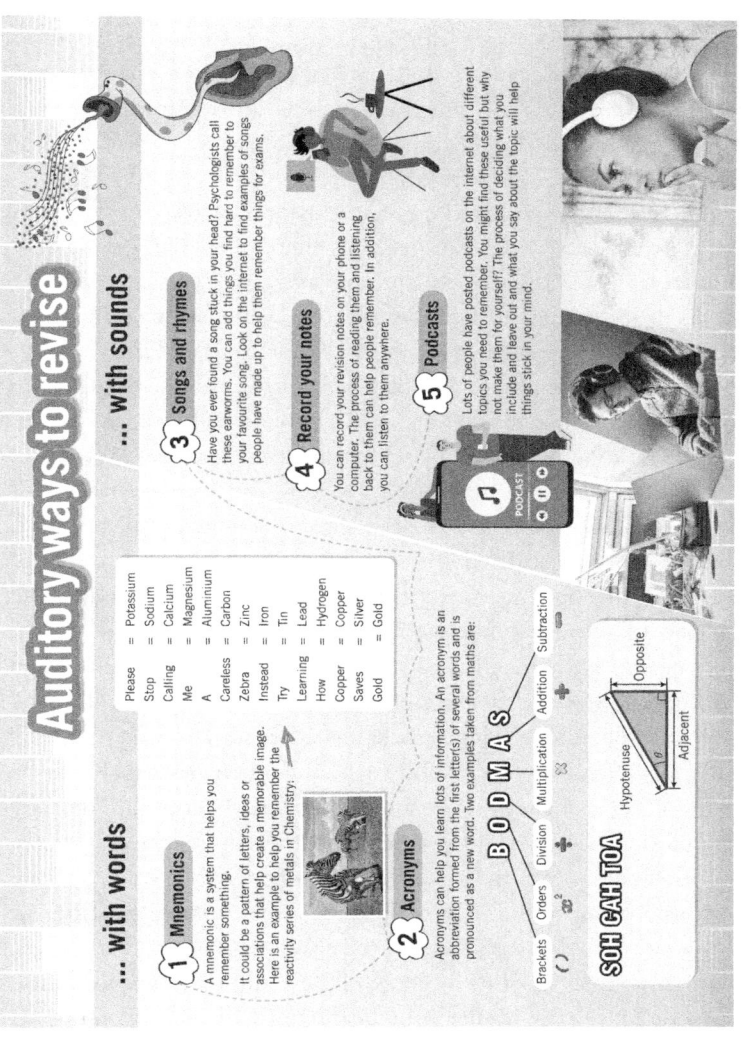

Figure 6.6 Auditory Ways to Revise.

When students come to revising and preparing for high-stakes exams, they can further reduce uncertainty by using a cycle of self-regulated learning. The principles of self-regulated learning were introduced by Barry Zimmerman (Zimmerman & Schunk, 2011). The basic idea is that students first plan and set learning goal and then engage in activities to meet these goals before reviewing whether those goals have been achieved. Then, new goals are set, and the cycle moves on as before.

The critical point when applying this framework to revision is that students set SMART goals (i.e., specific, measurable, achievable, relevant, and time-bound) and that revision is evaluated to provide feedback on whether it was effective or not in meeting goals. The idea of setting SMART goals can be incorporated into revision timetables and planning, rather than just setting aside a specific time (e.g., 30 minutes) to revise a particular subject and topic and to be very precise about what is to be achieved within that time. At the end of 30 minutes, or at some point afterwards, the goals are reviewed. Ultimately, the goal is to remember the curriculum/specification knowledge or skills that will be examined, so the best way to review goals is for the students to test themselves. This could be as simple as trying to write down everything that was remembered, telling someone else everything that was remembered, or practising a timed exam question. The latter option could be especially helpful if the student has been taught how marks are awarded.

If goals have been successfully achieved, then new goals can be set. If not, the student needs to judge why. Is another period of study required (i.e., is more time or practice that is required) or is the issue one of strategy (i.e., the strategy was ineffective)? If students have previously been shown how to judge the effectiveness of different study strategies, they may be able to make a more informed judgement. New goals need to be set, to repeat and the revision session should be repeated with the same or different strategy. Even if goals were met, it is also important to retest them in the future to check that goals can still be met and to consolidate knowledge and skills over time. Rarely is a single study session sufficient.

By working through a cycle of setting, testing, evaluating, and re-setting goals, students can provide themselves with ongoing feedback on the effectiveness of their revision and put themselves in a position to effect some changes if it is not effective. This approach will further reduce uncertainty and build confidence and control. Like test-taking strategies, some students will be able to adopt this approach on their own, whereas others will require support on how to set SMART goals, evaluate revision, and re-set goals.

REGULAR LOW-STAKES TESTING OF STUDENTS

Findings from the cognitive science literature show that regular testing is one of the most potent methods of consolidating knowledge and skills (Rowland, 2014). In addition to underpinning the regular revising and retesting of goals in a self-regulated cycle of learning, school and subject/curriculum leaders may wish to consider the regular regimes of low-stakes testing (e.g., once every four to six weeks or after every unit of work has been completed) prior to high-stakes exams. If students used effective revision and study strategies for these tests it would help strengthen long-term recall of knowledge and skills. Like the other test-taking and study-skills strategies I have described, it could help to reduce uncertainty and exam anxiety.

TEACHING STUDENTS PROGRESSIVE MUSCLE RELAXATION AND DIAPHRAGMATIC BREATHING

Two of the most popular physiological intervention strategies with students in STEPS are progressive muscle relaxation and diaphragmatic breathing (or, put more simply, deep breathing). These are popular with students as they are very quick and easy to learn, and in the case of diaphragmatic breathing (i.e., breathing from the diaphragm rather than the chest), can cause a strong anxiety reaction or panic attack or subside quickly. The latter can be a very useful strategy immediately prior to, or at the beginning of a high-stakes exam. There are no specific skills required to teach students these techniques, and there are numerous free instructional videos available online. This would make them, in my view, a time and cost-effective strategy for colleagues in schools and colleges to teach their students.

COMMUNICATION ABOUT HIGH-STAKES EXAMS

In Chapter 3, I suggested some ideas for how to talk to students about stress and the difference between threat and challenge responses to exam pressure. I would like to reiterate the point here that stress per se is not necessarily problematic if one responds to the pressure as a challenge. Staff in many schools and colleges will also talk to students in group settings (e.g., classes or assemblies) or provide information through official communications (e.g., email or newsletters) about the importance of high-stakes exams, the consequences of success and failure, how exam results can impact on future life trajectory, and the importance of preparing for exams as thoroughly as possible. I do not disagree with these messages. Indeed, school and college colleagues are alerting students to the reality of the situation they are in. Academic credentials have never been as important in the UK, and other countries, as they presently are for accessing education and training opportunities, and subsequent entry into the job market.

This is a topic I have conducted several studies into (Putwain et al., 2021), and it is important to bear in mind that within a group of typical students, there will be some who respond to messages like these as a challenge, others as a threat, while others actively choose to disregard the message (for numerous reasons). For some students, the message will act as the trigger for executive processes that could lead to ongoing cycles of exam anxiety as outlined in the S-REF model. It is not the message per se that is the issue, but that students can, and do, respond in very different ways.

The simplest recommendation is not to use these messages with groups of students but to personalise messages. I am not sure this is a practical suggestion, however, and it has somewhat utopian, dystopian, perhaps, overtones. A more practical suggestion, perhaps, is that whenever messages like these are given to students, they are accompanied by a very clear, explicit focus on skills and strategy. That is, what action students can take themselves in order to reduce uncertainty (e.g., test-taking skills and revision strategies) and manage anxiety (e.g., diaphragmatic breathing), and also to emphasise what support is being provided by the schools or college in order to help students as they prepare for and take high-stakes exams. The focus on skills and strategy will not stop a threat response in students but may help to reassure them. In short, I would encourage colleagues in schools and colleges to think carefullly about the tone and wording of messaging.

HOW CAN PARENTS AND CAREGIVERS SUPPORT HIGHLY EXAM-ANXIOUS STUDENTS?

Parental and caregiver support of high exam-anxious students is another area that has received little to no research attention. However, there are valuable insights provided through organisations like Parental Minds[13] who co-produce mental well-being support guides, using the experience of hundreds of families together with input from respected professionals and researchers. The insights contained in these guides can be usefully applied to exam anxiety. There are no magic solutions for parents that will 'fix' the issue of exam anxiety, and some of the recommendations I have made for schools and colleges, and in other parts of the book, are also relevant to parents. Nonetheless, there are some specific issues parents may face that I will outline below.

Dealing with a child or adolescent experiencing a high level of anxiety is itself an emotionally distressing and draining situation for parents and carers. It is important that if parents are feeling anxious, worried, or disappointed, for their child, to explain that it is not them but the situation. Furthermore, it is important for parents to avoid the trap of feeling guilty that they are to blame. Each child has their own unique genetic make-up, their own experiences, and their own life. These are not directly within parents' and caregivers' sphere of control. Parents can provide support and protection but cannot control life's experiences. Sometimes, parents stopping their own, or typical family activities, to provide their child with time may seem like the right thing to do, but it can result in them feeling guilty. It may not always be the right thing to do.

When discussing issues around exams and associated worries and anxieties, parents need to be silent to listen to their child properly and do not need to fix all their problems for them. Offer emotional support before jumping into problem solving, use compassionate language, and check first, if they do want problem-solving type help. It may be helpful to offer your own experiences (not necessarily about exams). For instance, that anxiety is an understandable reaction to some situations, that you and other people are also not happy all the time, experience worry and fear, and are sometimes sad and withdrawn. Parents can also consider their child's behaviour and whether any changes (e.g., becoming more withdrawn or irritable) and other emotions (e.g., lack of interest and enjoyment in usual activities) could be exam anxiety related. It is important parents acknowledge other emotions and behaviour, and not label it as anxiety-related on behalf of your child.

Finally, parents can take time to consider their own emotional state and own needs. People tend to relive important and/or difficult conversations with others afterwards in their own heads. Consider your own thoughts after a conversation about exams or exam anxiety with your child, which might include your own negative thoughts (e.g., "What if I hadn't said that?", "What else can I do?", "Why can't I stop my child's anxiety?", and "Could I have done more?"). If these thoughts are going through your head, you must challenge them (e.g., "Is that thought helpful?", "Is it accepting of the fact that I am not perfect (I am not a robot, I am a human being)?", "Is this thought true?", "Is it supportive of me and my child?", and "Am I trying to fix things rather than support my child?"). Parents can embrace the moments of joy with their child too, no matter how small or fleeting.

In addition to the advice offered by Parental Minds, there is also one point I would like to add. One of the reasons highly exam-anxious students perceive exams as threatening, as I explained in Chapter 1, is because they feel like they will be negatively judged by parents, or compared to other high achieving family members if they fail at exams or do not achieve a target or aspired for grade (Putwain, 2009). Psychologists call this 'mind reading' (a person believing that they know what or how others will think). Parents and carers can help to offset this worry by telling their children that they are valued and loved irrespective of their academic achievement. Of course, you might hope for and aspire for them to achieve highly, but the message is that you will not judge them negatively for not doing so. What you can praise is their effort or strategy rather than the outcome. Similarly, comparing the achievement of your children to other family members is to be avoided. It sends the message that achievement *is* something that you judge people by.

CHAPTER SUMMARY

In this chapter, I have outlined what can be done to support students who are highly exam-anxious. The positive message is that exam anxiety is extremely responsive to intervention. Although exam anxiety might be enduring, that does not mean it is not malleable. Interventions that are relatively brief and inexpensive are effective in reducing exam anxiety. I outlined two CBIs that focused on students aged 16–19 years. This does not mean these interventions are not of benefit to younger and older students. However, thought should be given to the appropriateness of the context of these interventions for different age groups. Younger students may benefit from a great focus on relaxation and diaphragmatic breathing, whereas university students may require less of a test-taking and study-skills focus. In addition, there are many ways that colleagues in schools and colleges can support students in simple and straightforward ways. Finally, I have summarised advice from Parental Minds, which may be useful if you have a highly exam-anxious child.

NOTES

1 An arbitrary rule of thumb for Glass' Δ, Cohen's *d*, and Hedge's *g*, is that an effect size >.2 is a small effect, >.5 is a moderate effect, and >.8 is a large effect. Some consider these rules of thumb controversial by some precisely because they are arbitrary. The sign of the effect size (+/−) indicates the direction of the difference between the intervention group compared to the control group or vice versa.

2 A type of behavioural treatment that involves graded exposure and relaxation to the threat situation (i.e., tests and exams).

3 For those interested in the technical difference, Glass's Δ standardises the difference in means between the intervention and control groups using the *standard deviation of the control group*. Cohen's *d* standardises the difference in means between the intervention and control groups using the *pooled standard deviation of the intervention and control groups*. Hedges *g* is similar to Cohen's *d* (i.e., based on pooled standard deviation) but accounts for sample sizes of the intervention and control groups.

4 Biofeedback involves learning to consciously control heart rate, blood pressure, and muscle tension.

5 Psychoeducation involves learning to identify triggers and signs of exam anxiety and understanding how cognitive, emotional, physiological, and behavioural factors interact in anxiety.

6 Cognitive bias modification is a procedure that trains attention away from threat stimuli. They often use an adapted dot probe task (see Chapter 5) where the arrow always replaces the non-threat stimuli.

7 Low intensity CBI is typically delivered by trained persons who do not have a core mental health qualification, with an emphasis on self-help, that typically involves six hours or less of contact time. Brief CBI can be of low or high intensity and refers to interventions that are typically 50% shorter (or more) than a full course of CBI (Shafran et al., 2021).

8 Universal interventions are offered to all students irrespective of risk or level of anxiety. In contrast, selective interventions are intended for students at elevated risk and targeted interventions for those at high risk.

9 Worry and tension scores were converted back to the scale metric of 1–4 (1 = never, 2 = sometimes, 3 = often, 4 = always; see Figure 2.2).

10 Like Putwain et al. (2014) worry and tension scores were converted back to the scale metric of 1–4 (1 = never, 2 = sometimes, 3 = often, 4 = always; see Figure 2.2).

11 In this context, I am using the term college to refer to 6th form college (i.e., academic upper secondary education) rather than university education.
12 To clarify, I am not implying learning styles (i.e., the widely discredited Visual-Auditory-Kinaesthetic model).
13 Parental Minds is a charity dedicated to empowering Caregivers who provide support to both adults and young people. They offer peer support and mentoring to caregivers, a service that provides a safety net of hope, and a team that remain alongside caregivers as often and as long as they need.

7

EDUCATIONAL POLICY
WHAT DOES THE FUTURE HOLD?

SETTING THE SCENE

As the wisdom of the ancient Greek philosopher Heraclitus goes, the only constant in life is change. As those who have worked in the UK school or higher education sectors in the last four decades will only know too well, this aphorism has never been truer than with educational policy.[1] Major curriculum and assessment initiatives within school settings have included the launch of the National Curriculum and associated National Curriculum Tests, and the General Certificate of Secondary Education (replacing the Certificate of Secondary Education and the General Certificate of Education: Ordinary Level), T-Levels, and the English Baccalaureate. These policies have centralised government control of the curriculum, its content, and its assessment. In doing so, it has been argued that the autonomy and professionalism of teachers have been undermined (Milner & Stevenson, 2019), and the role of the teacher is moving towards that of a civil servant charged with implementing government policy.

Top-down school accountability has been increased by making student performance on high-stakes exams publicly available through the Department of Education website and allowing custom tables to be created allowed for the comparison of schools within a specific local authority or geographical area.[2] In addition, a new school inspectorate was created, the Office for Standards in Education, Children's Services, and Skills (Ofsted) with wide-ranging powers for schools judged to be inadequate. These policies have been criticised for encouraging performativity and managerialism, and incentivising schools to become exam factories (Hutchings, 2015).

Within the higher education sector, the numbers of undergraduate students have risen sharply from the mid-1990s onwards, as have the numbers of overseas students and from the mid-2000s onwards. The cap for student tuition fees was raised to £9,000 in 2012 and £9250 in 2018, in England and Wales. Regulation and accountability initiatives were introduced through the Office for Students, the National Student Survey, the Teaching Excellent Framework, and the Research Excellence Framework. Students, it has been argued, are now positioned as consumers buying a higher education (Tomlinson, 2016). It is difficult not to imagine how the large debt incurred by students during the course of higher education[3] has not added to the pressures on them.

A full description of these policy changes and initiatives, the numerous others I have not mentioned, and an analysis of their effects are beyond the scope of this chapter. The point I want to make is that there have been wide-ranging and ongoing policy changes and initiatives that have impacted students, their teachers, and how educational institutions are organised and managed. The common theme is that these changes are driven by what is referred to as a neoliberal policy agenda. That is, to model public services on a market-driven model, reduce state interference, create systems of accountability, and promote choice. Given neoliberal policy is intended to reduce state interference, somewhat paradoxically, the opposite has happened.

EDUCATIONAL POLICY, EXAM ANXIETY, AND THE FUTURE

Successive government administrations in the UK since 1979 have pursued neoliberal policies with zeal. The devolved assemblies charged with educational policy in Northern Ireland, Scotland, and Wales do similarly, although there are important differences.[4] To a greater or lesser extent, most post-industrial nations also follow similar approaches (Prasad, 2006). Based on present political and policy discourse, I do not foresee a shift away from neoliberal policy in the UK or elsewhere.

The societal value attached to academic credentials has risen in tandem with these policy reforms. For example, schools in England are judged by Ofsted primarily on their academic results. Students in England who must legally remain in education until the age of 18 years, who did not achieve minimum pass grades in GCSE English and mathematics (secondary school-exit qualifications taken age 15–16 years) must retake these exams even if following vocational training routes or apprenticeships in areas such as hairdressing, vehicle repair and maintenance, construction, and health and beauty.[5] Jobs once seen as vocations (such as nursing) have been 'professionalised' by making their education and training routes undergraduate-level qualifications. Academic credentials are presented in both subtle and obvious ways as indispensable and quintessential.

It should come as no surprise that academic credentials assume value in the minds of young people. Their hegemony is all pervasive. Indeed, studies undertaken in the early 2000s by Michael Connor (2001, 2003) showed that teachers went to great lengths to shield pupils from the pressures associated with Year 6 National Curriculum Tests (NCTs) taken at the end of primary school aged 10–11 years.[6] Nonetheless, pupils themselves were acutely aware of their importance due to the frequency of practice tests, the emphasis on how to answer questions during lessons, how NCTs were talked about by teachers, and partly due to the lengths taken by teachers to shield pupils which paradoxically indicated their significance. Children are astute, and sadly, despite the best efforts of their teachers, some children became highly anxious about taking these tests (also see Hall et al., 2004).

Given the pervasiveness of academic credentials, the emphasis of schooling on *academic* achievement over other forms, especially during the latter years of secondary education, and the predominance of exam and test results as the principal indicator of academic achievement, it is not a surprise that children and young people come to accept that academic achievements, and test/exam results, are an important way in that people are judged. The process by which a person comes to accept the values of others, or social values, is called internalisation by psychologists. External values (i.e., dominant social narratives and the beliefs of influential others) become incorporated into a person's own values and beliefs such that the person comes to identify them as their own.

Through this process of internalisation, persons will come, to a greater or lesser extent, to judge themselves through their academic achievements (which is described in Marty Covington's self-worth theory, e.g., Covington, 2009). Of course, there are numerous factors that impact this process, including family background (and the associated cultural, economic, and social capital), friendship groups, interests, school experiences, teacher influences, personality characteristics, and so on. For those who do strongly internalise the value of academic credentials, the personal stakes are raised; pressure on oneself to achieve in order to experience positive self-worth judgements is increased. This is a double-edged sword. On the one hand, the person is highly motivated to achieve, but on the other, fear of failure is magnified.

Fear of failure alone may not be sufficient to give rise to persistent and excessive exam anxiety. Other factors specified in the S-REF Model (see Chapter 5), like cognitive biases, poor competence beliefs, ineffective coping strategies, and metacognitions about anxiety, also contribute. In addition, numerous studies conducted from the 1960s onwards show that students experienced high levels of exam anxiety prior to the pursuit of neoliberal educational policy, where, arguably, academic credentials were not quite so hegemonic. However, it is also difficult to foresee how there will be any change in the number of students experiencing severe exam anxiety that is damaging to their achievement, well-being, and health, while educational policy continues with its present focus on academic credentials and a narrow focus on academic achievement assessed through test and exam results.

One of the effects of the top-down accountability policies described by Merryn Hutchings (2015) is that schools and colleges have become like exam factories. That is, schools and colleges are heavily incentivised to prioritise the exam and test results of their students, leading to a narrowed curriculum, extra-curricular activities being reduced, and highly instrumental teaching of how to pass exams.[7] One might reasonably ask, what exactly is wrong with these accountability policies and focusing on academic achievement? Won't accountability policies drive up standards in schools[8] and academic achievement allows children and young people the opportunity to take pride in themselves and open up educational, training, and job opportunities that would otherwise be closed off?

This argument sounds plausible. There are downsides, however. One of them being that schools and teachers inadvertently become conduits, passing on the pressures that come with top-down accountability for students to achieve. The question we need to ask is whether children and young people need additional pressures coming downwards via policy, Ofsted, schools, and teachers, on top of the pressures that they experience from themselves, their families, and their peers. Furthermore, one may question whether this additional pressure may lead to longer-term health problems and alienate some persons from education rather than motivating and engaging them.

I argued in Chapter 3 that the issue is the not pressure itself but how one responds to that pressure. Persons who respond to pressure as a challenge can thrive. Those who respond to pressure as a threat struggle and may become anxious, with associated risks for lower well-being and poor mental health (see Chapter 4). That might be sufficient to argue for reducing pressure where possible. Long-term pressure is a different matter and can lead to a state of burnout characterised by emotional exhaustion, cynicism, and a loss of commitment, even in those who respond to acute pressure as a challenge. Burnout in students is, unsurprisingly, related to lower academic achievement (Madigan & Kim, 2021) and an increased risk of poor mental health (Walburg, 2014). Is the drive towards increasing achievement (i.e., test and exam grades) and school standards through top-down accountability policies worth the personal cost?

As many educationalists have reasoned (Lucey & Reay, 2002), the focus on academic achievement defacto involves failure for those who don't meet minimum grade or mark thresholds.[9] What effect might this have on a child or adolescent who repeatedly experiences educational failure within a classroom, school, and cultural milieu that adulates academic credentials? They learn that education and school is not for them, resulting in disengagement and disaffection. Strategies are employed to protect one's self-worth in the face of failure, such as strategic withdrawal of effort and self-sabotage. Some students may try to 'appear' engaged during lessons, so not to attract attention to themselves but are simply 'faking it' or superficially engaged. Others may engage in disruptive behaviour out of boredom or to deflect attention from their lack of interest in learning. In more extreme cases, the result is a complete alienation from education and school (Hascher & Haggenauer, 2010). Some would argue that the purpose of education (i.e., educere; to nurture and develop a person's interests and talents) has been seriously sidelined.

I have only briefly touched on some of the disadvantages of pursuing top-down accountability policies. There are numerous other ways in which they can detract from schooling and education and exert negative impacts on teachers as well as students. I would recommend readers who wish to explore these ideas in greater detail to read the work of Jane Perryman (Perryman et al., 2011), Stephen Ball (Ball, 2008), Diane Reay (Reay, 2010), and Sharon Nicols (Nichols & Berliner, 2007), as well as the 2015 'Exam Factories?' report by Merryn Hutchings.

WHAT CHANGES COULD BE MADE TO EDUCATIONAL POLICY TO BENEFIT STUDENT HIGHLY EXAM-ANXIOUS STUDENTS?

In contrast to the numerous studies investigating the personal psychological variables that impact exam anxiety, remarkably few studies have examined how qualification assessment structures, examination formats, and grading systems, could influence exam anxiety. What follows, therefore, are largely theoretically informed recommendations combined with the limited evidence that is available (see Howard, 2020, for a review of the evidence).

With regard to format, a single end-of-course exam inevitably results in greater pressure than several smaller exams that can be taken at intervals throughout a course.[10] In addition, modular exams that can be retaken before the end of a course will also reduce pressure as a student knows that a mark or grade that did not reach their aspiration is not final. Those who worked, or were students, in secondary and sixth-form education during the 2000s and 2010s in England, Wales, and Northern Ireland may recognise these approaches. Modular exams that could be retaken before the end of a course were routinely used for A-Level assessment and for several subjects in GCSE assessment.

Central government reforms in the 2010s returned to terminal exams due to concerns about grade inflation resulting from students repeatedly retaking modular exams to drive up grades and improve their academic standing. I find this concern strangely misplaced as schools were placed within an accountability system designed to incentivise schools to raise standards (i.e., test and exam grades). That is exactly what was done. Moreover, what exactly is wrong with grade inflation? If students (and their teachers) have worked hard enough to improve their results, why is that problematic?

My view is that concerns about grade inflation draw on a particular view about the purpose of education. If one believes the purpose of education is to differentiate between the more and less academically able (what some would describe as an elitist approach), then grade inflation is problematic. If there are too many students achieving high grades, differentiating them is not easy. There are, however, alternate views of education. If one believes the purpose of education is to create a workforce for the future, grade inflation is irrelevant. The focus is on whether students can demonstrate competencies in knowledge and skills required for different sectors of the job market. Similarly, if one views the purpose of education as identifying and nurturing interests and talent, grade inflation is an indifference.

Different views about the purpose of education also underlie approaches to grading. The norm-based approach, which adjusts grade boundaries to ensure only a certain proportion of students achieve the highest grades, clearly supports educational differentiation and can limit grade inflation. The criterion-based approach sets out the standards required for different grades. If a student meets those standards, they will be awarded a particular grade irrespective of how many other students also achieved that grade. For me, criterion-based approaches are a much fairer way to recognise student achievement.

Subjects that are awarded using a mixture of exams and coursework can also reduce exam pressures (although coursework can bring other pressures). Coursework was routinely used for GCSEs and A Levels before reforms in the 2010s due to concerns about plagiarism and a lack of standardisation over the level of assistance offered by teachers. Coursework was replaced with 'controlled assessments', namely tasks set by awarding bodies (e.g., translating text from one language to another in a foreign language subject or conducting a practical in a science subject) and conducted under time-limited supervised conditions with limited or no teacher assistance. Few studies have researched controlled assessments. One notable exception, by Rhian Barrance (2019), showed that teacher assistance remained inconsistent, and students were prepared for controlled assessments in the same way as exams, with a focus on memorisation. One might conclude that controlled assessments are more exam-like than coursework and do not reduce pressure on the student to the same degree.

I explained in Chapter 3 how exam anxiety can interfere with working memory capacity. Exams that involve answering questions with a high cognitive load may, therefore, be particularly difficult for highly exam-anxious students with an already depleted working memory. In addition, the anticipation of such questions (and the expectation of difficulty and, by implication, an increased likelihood of failure) could further increase pressures on highly exam-anxious students. Small steps to reduce cognitive load, for instance, by allowing formula sheets in mathematics and science will help to reduce pressure. Arguably, this may also assist in a more accurate assessment of subject-specific skills than one's ability to memorise.

Just as I only had the space to highlight a few of the ways in which educational policy can impact the pressures associated with taking exams, I have only the space to highlight how exam structure, format, and grading can impact exam pressures. In addition, it is important to highlight that while I focused on the disadvantages of policy reform with respect to exam pressure, there are potential advantages too. For those who would like to read further about policy changes in this area, and their advantages and disadvantages, I would suggest the 2019 report by Jo-Anne Baird and colleagues.

The aforementioned suggestions are all essentially ways to tinker within a system of top-down accountability through high-stakes testing and ubiquitous veneration of academic credentials. A far more radical proposition would be to stop using high-stakes exams altogether. Critics of examinations have often pointed out that written exams sat under standardised conditions to assess intelligence, ability, or a prescribed curriculum, became popularised in Victorian education in England primarily due to administrative reasons. They were easier to administer to large numbers of students, and subject specialists could design questions and marking schemes and ensure uniformity of questions and their presentation.[11]

The question I pose is whether administrative justifications are adequate for using exams as the principal method for assessing student achievement, given the consequences for their subsequent life trajectory, and judging school accountability. Might other methods provide a better assessment of students' knowledge, skills, and learning than exams? Essays, project work, lab work, and presentations (i.e., posters, blogs, and infographics) could provide alternates to exams. Indeed, such forms of assessment may facilitate greater student interest, motivation, and creativity than exams and offer a better fit to the skills required in the workplace. The difficulty is ensuring a degree of standardisation between teachers and schools to ensure students are operating on a level-playing field. An assessment system that was able to offer and monitor standardisation for non-exam assessments would be the ideal.

A second radical policy change would be to break the link between school accountability and results from high-stakes exams. That is, to judge school and teacher effectiveness using other means. Alternatives include a greater focus on the quality of planning, learning, and assessment, rather than test or exam outcomes, and a greater recognition of the expertise of teachers in making judgements about the appropriateness of teaching, learning, and assessment for particular groups of students. This need not rule out the use of tests per se, but it does require a change of use. A bank of tests developed collaboratively with teachers and school leaders could provide formative assessments at points when students are judged to be ready. School inspections can be retained but with a refined role in supporting school improvement and standards.

Some educationalists have questioned whether top-down accountability policies should be replaced with bottom-up systems where schools are accountable to the local community rather than central government. Key local stakeholders, which would include students or their advocates, would determine the specific outcomes on which schools should focus and be held accountable too. The goal is to align school accountability goals more clearly with the values and needs of students and their local community. I would refer readers who are interested to a series of proposals for the reforms of accountability in Primary education to a 2021 report by Gemma Moss.

WHAT CAN SCHOOLS DO AT PRESENT TO SUPPORT HIGHLY EXAM-ANXIOUS STUDENTS?

Crystal ball gazing and pontificating about policy change and where it might lead is fine. Back in the real world, however, working within policy constraints, I will conclude this chapter with nine suggestions about what schools can do to support students who have become severely anxious about exams. These points have already been made in previous chapters, but I hope that it will provide a useful summary by bringing them together in one place at the end of the book.

1. In secondary schools, normalise the theatre and ritual of taking exams in standardised settings (e.g., seated in rows, in silence, in a large hall). Begin this process earlier rather than later.
2. Discuss the issues around stress and exam anxiety in the appropriate forums. I would strongly encourage school leaders and staff to think about the most effective way to communicate the message that exam stress[12] is not something to be scared of and how stress can be utilised to improve motivation, effort, and performance.
3. Heavy-handed messages about the importance of exam grades for students' life trajectories may be true and may motivate some students. They are a risky strategy, however, and will act as an anxiety trigger for some students, resulting in the opposite outcome. Use with caution and ideally with individuals, not groups, and include reference to skills students can use to support learning, exam preparation, and anxiety management.
4. Teaching, learning, assessment, and exam preparation, strategies that enable students to build confidence and control in their academic ability *and* their ability to effect exam outcomes, will reduce anxiety. This may require explicit feedback by teachers to allow students to build control perceptions or students to reflect on their efforts and strategies to assess their strengths and weaknesses.
5. Allow students to try out, compare, and receive feedback (from teachers or self-assessed work), using different preparation strategies for low-stakes tests. This will help to ensure that students are using effective strategies and know that they are using them (and what alternates are available). This will help to build perceptions of control.

6. Using principles of self-regulated learning in exam preparation will assist in making preparation as effective as possible and build perceptions of confidence and control. Students will need to be supported through this process and require a lot of structure.
7. Do seek students' views about exam stress and anxiety. Many schools and colleges in the UK now routinely make use of surveys and champions to collect data on students' opinions about numerous elements of school life. Include exams, what kinds of support students would benefit from, how best to implement these supports, and how to discuss the importance of high-stakes exams most effectively and sensitively in student surveys and the like.
8. I would recommend using a standardised measurement of exam anxiety with robust psychometric properties like the MTAS (see Chapter 1). This could be administered alongside a student survey or as a standalone survey. It could be used as a 'temperature check' to establish levels of exam anxiety across a cohort of students or to identify those who may benefit from additional support and intervention. The MTAS could be used alongside other standardised measures of well-being and mental health to profile students (see Figure 2.5). This may assist the identification and differentiation of students in acute need of intervention and those who may benefit from more general stress and anxiety management advice.
9. Consider a targeted intervention for those students who are highly exam-anxious (e.g., like the CBIs described in Chapter 6). If these can be accommodated within school and college timetables, they are a high-gain, low-cost, evidence-based means of supporting students. Students could be identified through a mixture of teacher-referral, self-referral, and screening. Additional consideration should be given to providing a lower level of support for those students (e.g., a single session focusing on anxiety management strategies like diaphragmatic breathing and identifying and challenging automatic negative thoughts) with moderate to high levels of exam anxiety. Such an approach

to tiered intervention support could be informed by profiling students' exam anxiety, well-being, and mental health. The earlier that students can be identified and supported for intervention, the better. Ideally, intervention should not be left to the months immediately prior to high-stakes tests, or even the school year in which they are scheduled. Anecdotally, many schools in England struggle to support the number of requests they receive for exam accommodation of exam anxiety (e.g., to sit exams in a small room). One effective way to reduce requests for exam accommodations for exam anxiety would be to intervene as early as possible to provide students with the skills to manage their anxiety effectively.

CHAPTER SUMMARY

This concluding chapter has considered some of the ways in which the broader educational policy has provided fertile ground for exam anxiety to thrive. The focus on academic credentials, judging academic achievement in terms of test and exam scores, and top-down school accountability is unlikely to change in the near future.[13] That does not mean, however, that there are no practical steps that can be taken by schools, teachers, and not least students themselves, to help manage and reduce exam anxiety. Even if policy changes were made, some students would inevitably still become highly exam-anxious.

Some school and teacher strategies could be routinely incorporated into existing planning for teaching and learning (e.g., experimenting with different approaches to exam preparation in low-stakes tests). Others, like screening and intervention, may require changes of practice to incorporate them into planning and timetabling. The point I would like to finish on is, I hope, a positive one. Severe exam anxiety is something experienced by many children and young people. It is, however, something that can be effectively managed with relatively brief intervention, and students can be supported in numerous other ways. Severe exam anxiety is not an inevitability. As parents, teachers, researchers, and professionals working to support the learning, well-being, and mental health of children and young people, I would argue we have a duty to help make interventions and other forms of support as widely accessible as possible.

NOTES

1 Other countries have undergone major education policy reforms like No Child Left Behind (and the associated use of high-stakes testing) and the Common Core Standards Initiative in the United States.
2 Initially, the Department for Education grouped schools by locality. The resultant tables were referred to in colloquial terms, using a sporting analogy, as 'league tables'. Now that the user can choose their own geographical parameters of comparison schools, I do not think the analogy works so well.
3 The average debt for a student on graduation for a student starting an undergraduate degree in 2023/2024 is £42,900 (Bolton, 2023). Interest is added at 9% per annum. The average student debt in England and Wales is the highest for any OECD nation (OECD, 2022).
4 For example, students are not charged university tuition fees in Northern Ireland and Scotland; school inspections are organised differently in Northern Ireland, Scotland, and Wales. It could be argued that neoliberal policy in the UK has been pursued most acutely in England.
5 Students without minimum pass grades in English and mathematics would not typically be accepted for academic upper-secondary education.
6 Often referred to as standard assessment tasks (SATs) for reasons I have never been able to work out.
7 Which, it should be noted, that I suggested in Chapter 6 might be of particular benefit to highly exam-anxious students.
8 The standard response of politicians who support and implement neo-liberal education policy is a rhetorical fallacy if I have ever heard one. One cannot argue against the principle of driving up standards, but *it is possible* to judge this not solely based on test and exam results.
9 This is exacerbated when grading assumes an underlying normal distribution and grade boundaries are adjusted to fit this distribution (sometimes referred to as grading on a curve) where ≈50% of scores will

be below the mean. One would expect this reasoning to pose a quandary for Michael Gove (English Secretary of State for Education 2010 to 2014: https://publications.parliament.uk/pa/cm201012/cmselect/cmeduc/uc1786-i/uc178601.htm).
10 In the UK, the parlance is 'terminal' or 'linear' for end-of-course exams and 'modular' for those taken at intervals.
11 Those who make the claim that the Victorian comparison is 'lazy' perhaps might first like to read "Examining the world: A history of The University of Cambridge Local Examinations Syndicate" by Sandra Raban (2008) and "Making a Grade: Victorian Examinations and the Rise of Standardized Testing" by James Elwick (2021). In doing so, they make discover the indolent nature of their claim.
12 Acute rather than chronic stress.
13 I hope that I am wrong.

GLOSSARY

Academic Self-Efficacy A person's belief that they can successfully complete a forthcoming task (conceptually very similar to expectancy of success).

Academic Self-Concept A person's judgement of their competence in a specific academic subject/domain, or school in general.

Academic Self-Handicapping See self-sabotage.

Attentional Control Theory A type of cognitive interference theory that proposes anxiety interferes with working memory resources to reduce task efficiency but not necessarily task performance.

Challenge State When persons respond to stressors (demands) as a challenge resulting in positive emotions (like hope), motivation, and effort.

Coping The adaptive and maladaptive strategies used in response to stressors (demands).

Cognitive Affective Syndrome A style of thinking characterised by inflexible and ruminative styles of thinking about negative beliefs, feelings, and thoughts, that results in emotional distress.

Cognitive-Behavioural Intervention (CBI) A type of psychological intervention that involves learning strategies to relax, control physiological reactions to anxiety, overcome avoidance behaviours, and challenge cognitive biases and unhelpful metacognitive beliefs about anxiety.

Cognitive Biases Beliefs that magnify threat or hopelessness to maintain or amplify anxiety and depression.

Cognitive Distortions See cognitive biases.

Cognitive Interference Theories A group of theories that describe how anxiety interferences with working memory leading to a potential decline in task performance.

Cognitive Load Theory A theory to describe how task performance depends on the balance between demands made on working memory resources and working memory capacity.

Control Beliefs When a student is confident that they know how to obtain success and avoid failure (related to academic self-efficacy and academic self-concept).

Criterion-Referencing A standard is derived from a set of prior agreed benchmarks.

Effect Size A statistic to represent the size of a relation between two or more variables, or the difference between two or more groups.

Ego Threat The psychological threat posed by an event to one's sense of self-worth or self-esteem.

Emotion Disorder An omnibus term for anxiety disorders and depression.

Eudaimonic Well-Being Finding meaning and purpose in one's life, including personal growth, environmental mastery, positive relationships, autonomy, and self-actualisation.

Executive Processes The psychological term given to the conscious and deliberate direction of attention to external or internal stimuli.

Externalising Disorder A group of disorders characterised by symptoms turned outwardly (e.g., antisocial behaviour).

Generalised Anxiety Disorder A clinical anxiety disorder characterised by worry, fatigue, irritability, and trouble sleeping.

General Certificate of Secondary Education (GCSE) Qualifications in different subjects awarded at the end of secondary school (aged 15–16 years) in England, Wales, and Northern Ireland.

General Certificate of Education: Advanced Level (A Level) Qualifications in different subjects awarded at the end of upper secondary education (aged 17–18 years) in England, Wales, and Northern Ireland.

Hedonic Well-Being Life satisfaction together with the presence of positive mood and the absence of negative mood.

Internalising Disorder A group of disorders (including anxiety, depression, and eating disorders) characterised by symptoms turned inwardly (e.g., emotional distress).

Major Depression A depressed mood or a marked loss of interest and enjoyment in usual activities for a discrete period.

National Student Survey An annual survey of all students in higher education about their satisfaction with the courses, teaching staff, and institution.

Meta-Analysis An analysis that uses findings from multiple studies to establish effects or relations based on a larger and often more diverse range of participants and contexts.

Metacognitive Beliefs These are beliefs about beliefs or one's mental state (e.g., beliefs about whether anxiety is harmful, controllable).

National Curriculum Tests Tests taken by students in English Primary Schools in Years 2 (aged 6–7 years) and 6 (aged 10–11 years).

Neoliberal Policy. To model public services, including education using market-driven principles.

Normal Distribution A distribution in which the mean, median, and mode lie at the same point resulting in 50% of scores above, and 50% below the mean.

Norm-Referencing A standard is derived in relation to the scores of other persons.

Nosological Classification of Mental Disorders Classifying poor mental health into different disorders each with unique symptoms, causes, and outcomes, and which respond to different treatments.

Office for Standards in Education, Children's Services, and Skills (Ofsted) The school inspectorate in England.

Office for Students The regulator of higher education in England.

Panic Disorder A clinical anxiety disorder characterised by intense episodes of a rapid pounding heart, trembling or shaking, shortness of breath, and a feeling of impending doom or danger.

Performance-Evaluative Situation A situation in which one's performance is evaluated.

Procrastination Putting something off until an undefined later point in time.

Research Excellence Framework A periodic review of the quality of research undertaken in British higher education institutions through outputs (i.e., journal articles), the non-academic impact of research (i.e., social or economic impact), and research environment. Results determine direct government allocation of research funding.

Self-Regulation The positive and negative strategies people use to monitor and control their cognition, emotion, and behaviour.

Separation Anxiety Disorder Inappropriate and excessive fear of separation from those to whom an individual is attached.

Self-Referent Executive Function Model A psychological model of emotional distress that emphasises metacognitive beliefs as underling maladaptive and unhelpful coping approaches that develop or maintain anxiety.

Self-Sabotage Deliberately creating obstacles to academic success to increase the likelihood of failure; a method of deflecting the reasons for failure away from one's competence to protect self-worth or self-esteem.

Sixth Form A colloquial term for academic upper secondary education in England, Wales, and Northern Ireland.

Social Anxiety Disorder An intense fear of being scrutinised by others in social situations and showing anxiety will result in embarrassment or rejection by others.

Specific Phobia A persistent, intense, and disproportionate, fear of specific object or situation.

Statistical Significance The probability (*p*) of not finding the same result from another randomly sampled group from the same (statistical) population of participants.

Stress A situation judged to be personally meaningful which requires action on the part of the person to ensure their goals are met. Can be judged as a challenge or a threat.

State Anxiety The level and intensity of anxiety experienced at any given moment.

Subjective Well-being See hedonic well-being.

Systematic Review A summary of a group of studies that are chosen on a specific set of criteria.

Teaching Excellence Framework The Office for Students awards higher education institutions categories of gold, silver, and bronze, for the perceived quality of teaching, learning, and student outcomes (e.g., in employment or further study). It is based on part of responses to the National Student Survey.

Transdiagnostic Approaches to Mental Disorders A group of approaches that use broader categories of mental health (e.g., externalising and internalising disorders) than traditional nosological approaches.

Threat State When persons respond to stressors (demands) as a threat resulting in negative emotions (like anxiety) and avoidance responses.

Trait Anxiety Individual differences in the general tendency towards experiencing state anxiety.

Uncertain Control When a student does not know why they obtained a particular score or grade (i.e., success or failure).

Working Memory The cognitive resource used to consciously hold, process, and manipulate temporary information.

Yerkes–Dodson Law The idea that the relation between arousal and performance is curvilinear and follows an upside down U shape; performance improves with low to moderate arousal and declines with moderate to high arousal.

Z-Score A score on a scale is transformed into standardised units (i.e., standard deviations).

FURTHER READING

Cassady, J.C. (2004). The influence of cognitive test anxiety across the learning–testing cycle. *Learning and Instruction, 14,* 569–592. https://doi.org/10.1016/j.learninstruc.2004.09.002

Ergene, T. (2003). Effective interventions for test anxiety reduction. *School Psychology International, 24,* 313–328. https://doi.org/10.1177/01430343030243004

Flaxman, P.E., Bond, F.W., & Keogh, E. (2003). Preventing and treating evaluation strain: A technically eclectic approach. In F.W. Bond & W. Dryden (Eds.), *Handbook of brief cognitive-behavior therapy* (pp. 239–288). John Wiley & Sons.

Hembree, R. (1988). Correlates, causes, effects and treatment of test anxiety. *Review of Educational Research, 58,* 47–77. https://doi.org/10.3102/00346543058001047

Hutchings, M. (2015). *Exam factories? The impact of accountability measures on children and young people.* National Union of Teachers.

Khng, K.H. (2017). A better state-of-mind: deep breathing reduces state anxiety and enhances test performance through regulating test cognitions in children. *Cognition and Emotion, 31,* 1502–1510. https://doi.org/10.1080/02699931.2016.1233095

Matthews, G., Hillyard, E.J., & Campbell, S.E. (1999). Metacognition and maladaptive coping as components of test anxiety. *Clinical Psychology and Psychotherapy, 6,* 111–125. https://doi.org/ 10.1002/(SICI)1099-0879(199905)

Putwain, D.W. (2020). *Examination pressures on children and young people: Are they taken seriously enough?* The British Academy.

Putwain, D.W., & Pescod, M. (2018). Is reducing uncertain control the key to successful test anxiety for Secondary school students? Findings from a randomized control trial. *School Psychology Quarterly, 33*, 283–292. https://doi.org/10.1037/spq0000228

Putwain, D.W., & von der Embse, N.P. (2021). Cognitive-behavioural intervention for test anxiety in adolescent students: Do benefits extend to school-related wellbeing and clinical anxiety. *Anxiety, Stress, and Coping, 34*, 22–36. https://doi.org/10.1080/10615806.2020.1800656

Robson, D.A., Johnstone, S.J., Putwain, D.W., & Howard, S. (2023). Test anxiety in primary school children: A 20-year systematic review and meta-analysis. *Journal of School Psychology, 98*, 39–60. https://doi.org/10.1016/j.jsp.2023.02.003

Soares, D., & Woods, K. (2020). An international systematic literature review of test anxiety interventions 2011–2018. *Pastoral Care in Education, 38*(4), 311–334, https://doi.org/10.1080/02643944.2020.1725909

Spielberger, C.D., & Vagg, R.P. (1995). Test anxiety: A transactional process model. In C.D. Speilberger & P.R. Vagg (Eds.), *Test Anxiety: Theory, Assessment and Treatment* (pp. 3–14). Taylor & Francis.

Travis, J., Kaszycki, A., Geden, M., & Bunde, J. (2020). Some stress Is good stress: The challenge-hindrance framework, academic self-efficacy, and academic outcomes. *Journal of Educational Psychology, 112*, 1632–1643. https://doi.org/10.1037/edu0000478

von der Embse, N., Barterian, J., & Segool, N. (2013). Test anxiety interventions for children and adolescents: A systematic review of treatment studies from 2000–2010. *Psychology in the Schools, 50*, 57–71. https://doi.org/10.1002/pits.21660

von der Embse, N.P., Jester, D., Roy, D., & Post, J. (2018). Test anxiety effects, predictors, and correlates: A 30-year meta-analytic review. *Journal of Affective Disorders, 227*, 483–493. https://doi.org/10.1016/j.jad.2017.11.048

Wells, A. (2009). *Metacognitive therapy for anxiety and depression.* Guilford Press.

Wells, A., & Matthews, G. (1996). Modelling cognition in emotional disorder: The S-REF model. *Behaviour Research and Therapy, 34*, 881–888. https://doi.org/10.1016/S0005-7967(96)00050-2

Yeo, L.S., Goh, V.G., & Liem, G.A.D. (2016). School-based intervention for test anxiety. *Child & Youth Care Forum, 45*, 1–17. https://link.springer.com/article/10.1007/s10566-015-9314-1

Zeidner, M. (1998). *Test anxiety: The state of the art.* Plenum.

Zeidner, M. (2007). Test anxiety in educational contexts: Concepts, findings and future directions. In P.A. Schutz & R. Pekrun (Eds.), *Emotion in education* (pp. 165–184). Elsevier.

Zeidner, M. (2014). Anxiety in education. In R. Pekrun & L. Linnenbrink-Garcia (Eds.), *International handbook of emotions in education* (pp. 265–288). Routledge.

Zeidner, M., & Matthews, G. (2005). Evaluation anxiety. In A.J. Elliot & C.S. Dweck (Eds.), *Handbook of competence and motivation* (pp. 141–163). Guilford Press.

REFERENCES

American Educational Research Association, American Psychological Association, & National Council on Measurement in Education. (2014). *Standards for educational and psychological testing*. American Educational Research Association.

American Psychiatric Association. (2022). *Diagnostic and statistical manual of mental disorders* (5th Edition, Text Revision). American Psychiatric Publishing.

Baird, J.-A., Caro, D., Elliott, V., El Masri, Y., Ingram, J., Isaacs, T., Pinot de Moira, A., Randhawa, A., Stobart, G., Meadows, M., Morin, C., & Taylor, R. (2019). *Examination reform: Impact of linear and modular examinations at GCSE*. Ofqual.

Ball, S.J. (2008). *The education debate*. Policy Press.

Barrance, R. (2019). The fairness of internal assessment in the GCSE: The value of students' accounts. *Assessment in Education: Principles, Policy & Practice*, 26(5), 563–583. https://doi.org/10.1080/0969594X.2019.1619514

Beck, A.T. (1979). *Cognitive therapy and the emotional disorders*. Penguin.

Beck, K.C., Røhr, H.L., Reme, B.-A., & Flatø, M. (2023). Distressing testing: A propensity score analysis of high-stakes exam failure and mental health. *Child Development*, 95(1), 242–260. https://doi.org/10.1111/cdev.13985

Bosman, R.C., Ten Have, M., de Graaf, R., Muntingh, A.D., Van Balkom, A.J., & Batelaan, N.M. (2019). Prevalence and course of subthreshold anxiety disorder in the general population: A three-year follow-up study. *Journal of Affective Disorders, 247*, 105–113. https://doi.org/10.1016/j.jad.2019.01.018

Bitsko, R.H., Claussen, A.H., Lichstein, J., Black, L.I., Jones, S.E., Danielson, M.L., ... Meyer, L.N. (2022). Mental health surveillance among children – United States, 2013–2019. *Morbidity and Mortality Weekly Report Supplements, 71*(2), 1–42. https://doi.org/10.15585/mmwr.su7102a1

Bolton, P. (2023). *Student load statistics: House of commons library research briefing (CBP01079)*. HMSO.

Broadhurst, P.L. (1959). The interaction of task difficulty and motivation: The Yerkes Dodson law revived. *Acta Psychologica, 16*, 321–338. https://doi.org/10.1016/0001-6918(59)90105-2

British Psychological Society. (2023). *Strategies to tackle exam pressure and stress: Revision guide*. British Psychological Society.

Burcaş, S., & Creţu, R.Z. (2020). Multidimensional perfectionism and test anxiety: A meta-analytic review of two decades of research. *Educational Psychology Review, 33*, 249–273. https://doi.org/10.1007/s10648-020-09531-3

Carver, C.S., Scheier, M.F., & Weintraub, J.K. (1989). Assessing coping strategies: A theoretically based approach. *Journal of Personality and Social Psychology, 56*(2), 267–283. http://dx.doi.org/10.1037//0022-3514.56.2.267

Cassady, J.C., Helsper, A., & Quagliano, Q. (2024). The collective influence of intolerance of uncertainty, cognitive test anxiety, and academic self-handicapping on learner outcomes: Evidence for a process model. *Behavioral Sciences, 14*(2), 96. https://doi.org/10.3390/bs14020096

Chaplin, T.M., & Aldao, A. (2013). Gender differences in emotion expression in children: A meta-analytic review. *Psychological Bulletin, 139*(4), 735–765. https://doi.org/10.1037/a0030737

Cohen, J. (1988). *Statistical power analysis for the behavioral sciences* (2nd Edition). Laurence Erlbaum Associates.

Connor, M.J. (2001). Pupil stress and standard assessment tests (SATS). *Emotional and Behavioural Difficulties, 6*(2), 103–111. http://dx.doi.org/10.1080/13632750300507010

Connor, M.J. (2003). Pupil stress and standard assessment tests (SATS): An update. *Emotional and Behavioural Difficulties, 8*(2), 101–107. https://doi.org/10.1080/13632750300507010

Cortina, M., Linehan, T., & Sheppard, K. (2021). *Working towards mentally healthy schools and FE colleges: The voice of students*. Anna Freud Centre.

REFERENCES

Covington, M. (2009). Self-worth theory: Retrospects and prospects. In K.R. Wentzel & A. Wigfield (Eds.), *Handbook of motivation at school* (pp. 141–170). Routledge.

Dalgleish, T., Black, M., Johnston, D., & Bevan, A. (2020). Transdiagnostic approaches to mental health problems: Current status and future directions. *Journal of Consulting and Clinical Psychology, 88*(3), 179–195. https://doi.org/10.1037/ccp0000482

DeCoster, J., Iselin, A.M.R., & Gallucci, M. (2009). A conceptual and empirical examination of justifications for dichotomization. *Psychological Methods, 14*(4), 349. https://doi.org/10.1037/a0016956

Diener, E., Lucas, R.E., Oishi, S., Hall, N., & Donnellan, M.B. (2018). Advances and open questions in the science of subjective well-being. *Collabra: Psychology, 4*(1), 1–49. https://doi.org/10.1525/collabra.115

Eccles, J.S., & Wigfield, A. (2020). From expectancy-value theory to situated expectancy-value theory: A developmental, social cognitive, and sociocultural perspective on motivation. *Contemporary Educational Psychology, 61*, 101859. https://doi.org/10.1016/j.cedpsych.2020.101859

Elwisk, J. (2021). *Making a grade: Victorian examinations and the rise of standardized testing*. University of Toronto Press.

Endler, N.S., & Parker, J.D.A. (1994). Assessment of multidimensional coping: Task, emotion, and avoidance strategies. *Psychological Assessment, 6*(1), 50–60. https://doi.org/10.1037/1040-3590.6.1.50

Ergene, T. (2003). Effective interventions for test anxiety reduction. *School Psychology International, 24*(3), 313–328. https://doi.org/10.1177/01430343030243004

Eysenck, M.W., Derakshan, N., Santos, R., & Calvo, M.G. (2007). Anxiety and cognitive performance: Attentional control theory. *Emotion, 7*(2), 336–353. https://doi.org/10.1037/1528-3542.7.2.336

Fenouillet, F., Nelson, V., Lorant, S., Masson, J., & Putwain, D.W. (2023). French study of multidimensional test anxiety scale in relation to performance, age and gender. *Journal of Psychoeducational Assessment, 41*(7), 828–834. https://doi.org/10.1177/07342829231186876

Folkman, S., & Lazarus, R.S. (1985). If it changes it must be a process: Study of emotion and coping during three stages of a college examination. *Journal of Personality and Social Psychology, 48*(1), 150–170. https://doi.org/10.1037/0022-3514.48.1.150

GBD 2019 Mental Disorders Collaborators. (2022). Global, regional, and national burden of 12 mental disorders in 204 countries and territories, 1990–2019: A systematic analysis from the Global Burden of Disease Study 2019. *The Lancet Psychiatry, 9*, 137–150. https://doi.org/10.1016/S2215-0366(21)00395-3

Hall, K., Collins, C., Benjamin, S., Nind, M., & Sheehy, K. (2004). SATurated models of pupildom: Assessment and inclusion/exclusion. *British Educational Research Journal, 30*(6), 801–881. https://doi.org/10.1080/0141192042000279512

Hagtvet, K.A., & Benson, J. (1997). The motive to avoid failure and test anxiety responses: Empirical support for integration of two research traditions. *Anxiety, Stress and Coping, 10*(1), 35–37. https://doi.org/10.1080/10615809708249294

Hascher, T., & Hagenauer, G. (2010). Alienation from school. *International Journal of Educational Research, 49*(6), 220–232. https://doi.org/10.1016/j.ijer.2011.03.002

Hembree, R. (1988). Correlates, causes, effects, and treatment of test anxiety. *Review of Educational Research, 58*(1), 47–77. https://doi.org/10.2307/1170348

Helzer, J.E., Wittchen, H.U., Krueger, R.F., & Kraemer, H.C. (2007). Dimensional options for DSM-V: The way forward. In Helzer, J.E., Kraemer, H.C., Krueger, R.F., Wittchen, H.U., Sirovatka, P.J., & Regier, D.A. (Eds.), *Dimensional approaches in diagnostic classification: Refining the research agenda for DSM-V* (pp. 115–127). American Psychiatric Association.

Herzer, F., Wendt, J., & Hamm, A.O. (2014). Discriminating clinical from nonclinical manifestations of test anxiety: A validation study. *Behavior Therapy, 45*(2), 222–231. https://doi.org/10.1016/j.beth.2013.11.001

Higa-McMillan, C.K., Frances, S.E., Rith-Najarian, L., & Chorpita, B.F. (2016). Evidence base update: 50 years of research on treatment for child and adolescent anxiety. *Journal of Clinical Child and Adolescent Psychology, 45*(2), 91–113. https://doi.org/10.1080/15374416.2015.1046177

Högberg, B., & Horn, D. (2022). National high-stakes testing, gender, and school stress in Europe: A difference-in-differences analysis. *European Sociological Review, 38*, 975–987. https://doi.org/10.1093/esr/jcac009

Högberg, B., Strandh, M., & Hagquist, C. (2020). Gender and secular trends in adolescent mental health over 24 years – the role of school-related stress. *Social Science Medicine, 250.* 112890. https://doi.org/10.1016/j.socscimed.2020.112890

Howard, E. (2020). *A review of the literature concerning anxiety for educational assessments.* His Majesties Stationary Office.

Hu, C., Oei, T.P., Huang, Q., & Zhou, R. (2023). Early vigilance and improved processing efficiency to the test-related target in test anxiety: Evidence from the visual search task and eye-movements. *Current Psychology, 42,* 11661–11673. https://doi.org/10.1007/s12144-021-02454-4

Huntley, C., Young, B., Tudur Smith, C., Jha, V., & Fisher, P. (2022). Testing times: The association of intolerance of uncertainty and metacognitive beliefs to test anxiety in college students. *BMC Psychology, 10*(1). https://doi.org/10.1186/S40359-021-00710-

Huntley, C.D., Young, B., Temple, J., Longworth, M., Smith, C.T., Jha, V., & Fisher, P.L. (2019). The efficacy of interventions for test anxious university students: A meta-analysis of randomized controlled trials. *Journal of Anxiety Disorders, 63,* 36–50. https://doi.org/10.1016/j.janxdis.2019.01.007

Huntley, C.D., Young, B., Tudur Smith, C., & Fisher, P.L. (2023). Metacognitive beliefs predict test anxiety and examination performance. *Frontiers in Education, 8,* 1051304. https://doi.org/10.3389/feduc.2023.1051304

Hutchings, M. (2015). *Exam factories? The impact of accountability measures on children and young people.* National Union of Teachers.

Jastrowski Mano, K.E., Gibler, R.C., Mano, Q.R., & Beckmann, E. (2018). Attentional bias toward school-related academic and social threat among test-anxious undergraduate students. *Learning and Individual Differences, 64,* 138–146. https://doi.org/10.1016/j.lindif.2018.05.003

Keeley, J., Zayac, R., & Correia, C. (2008). Curvilinear relationships between statistics anxiety and performance among undergraduate students: Evidence for optimal anxiety. *Statistics Education Research Journal, 7*(1), 4–15. https://doi.org/10.52041/serj.v7i1.477

Keith, T.Z. (2006). *Multiple regression and beyond.* Pearson Education.

Keith, T.Z. (2015). *Multiple regression and beyond: An introduction to multiple regression and structural equation modeling* (2nd Edition). Taylor & Francis.

King, N.J., Mietz, A., Tinney, L., & Ollendick, T.H. (1995). Psychopathology and cognition in adolescents experiencing severe test anxiety. *Journal of Clinical Child Psychology, 24,* 49–54. https://doi.org/10.1207/s15374424jccp2401_6.

King, R.B., Cai, Y., & Elliot, A.J. (2024). Income inequality is associated with heightened test anxiety and lower academic achievement: A cross-national study in 51 countries. *Learning and Instruction*, *89*, 101825. https://doi.org/10.1016/j.learninstruc.2023.101825

Kondaš, O. (1967). Reduction of examination anxiety and 'stage-fright' by group desensitization and relaxation. *Behaviour Research and Therapy*, *5*(4), 275–281.https://doi.org/10.1016/0005-7967(67)90019-8

LeBeau, R.T., Glenn, D., Liao, B., Wittchen, H., Beesdo-Baum, K., Ollendick, T., & Craske, M.G. (2010). Specific phobia: A preliminary review of DSM-IV specific phobia and preliminary recommendations for DSM-V. *Depression and Anxiety*, *27*, 148–167. https://doi.org/10.1002/da.20655

Lovett, B.J., Nelson, J.M., & O'Meara, P. (2024). Test anxiety symptoms in college students: Base rates and statistical deviance. *Psychological Injury and Law*. Advance Online Publication. https://doi.org/10.1007/s12207-023-09494-0

Lucey, H., & Reay, D. (2002). Carrying the beacon of excellence: Social class differentiation and anxiety at a time of transition. *Journal of Education Policy*, *17*(3), 321–336. https://doi.org/10.1080/02680930210127586

Madigan, D.J., & Kim, L.E. (2021). Does teacher burnout affect students? A systematic review of its association with academic achievement and student-reported outcomes. *International Journal of Educational Research*, *105*, 101714. https://doi.org/10.1016/j.ijer.2020.101714

Marsh, H.W., Pekrun, R., Parker, P.D., Murayama, K., Guo, J., Dicke, T., & Arens, A.K. (2019). The murky distinction between self-concept and self-efficacy: Beware of lurking jingle-jangle fallacies. *Journal of Educational Psychology*, *111*(2), 331–353. https://doi.org/10.1037/edu0000281

McDonald, A.S. (2001). The prevalence and effects of test anxiety in school children. *Educational Psychology*, *21*(1), 89–101. https://doi.org/10.1080/01443410020019867

McLean, C.P., & Anderson, E.R. (2009). Brave men and timid women? A review of the gender differences in fear and anxiety. *Clinical Psychology Review*, *29*(6), 496–505. https://doi.org/10.1016/j.cpr.2009.05.003

Messick, S. (1995). Standards of validity and the validity of standards in performance assessment. *Educational Measurement: Issues and Practice*, *14*(4), 5–8. https://doi.org/10.1111/j.1745-3992.1995.tb00881.x

Milner, A.L., & Stevenson, H. (2019). Teacher professionalism in England: Teachers' work at the sharp end of neoliberal education reform. In S. Chitpin & J.P. Portelli (Eds.), *Confronting educational policy in neoliberal times: International perspectives* (pp. 101–114). Routledge.

Moran, T.P. (2016). Anxiety and working memory capacity: A meta-analysis and narrative review. *Psychological Bulletin, 142*(8), 831–864. https://doi.org/10.1037/bul0000051

Moss, G., Goldstein, H., Hayes, S., Chereau, B.M., Sammons, P., Sinnott, G., & Stobart, G. (2021). *High standards, not high stakes: An alternative to SATs that will transform England's testing & school accountability system in primary education & beyond.* British Educational Research Association. https://www.bera.ac.uk/publication/high-standards-not-high-stakes-an-alternative-to-sats

Nichols, S.L., & Berliner, D.C. (2007). *Collateral damage: How high-stakes testing corrupts America's schools.* Harvard Education Press.

Nottelmann, E.D., & Hill, K.T. (1977). Test anxiety and off-task behavior in evaluative situations. *Child Development, 48*(1), 225–231. https://doi.org/10.2307/1128902

OECD. (2017). PISA 2015 results (volume III): Students' well-being. OECD Publishing. https://doi.org/10.1787/9789264273856-en

OECD. (2022). *Education at a glance 2022: OECD indicators.* OECD Publishing. https://doi.org/10.1787/3197152b-en

Owens, M., Stevenson, J., Norgate, R., & Hadwin, J.A. (2008). Processing efficiency theory in children: Working memory as a mediator between trait anxiety and academic performance. *Anxiety, Stress, & Coping, 21*(4), 417–430. https://doi.org/10.1080/10615800701847823

Pearson. (2021). *Mathematics paper 1 (non-calculator) higher tier.* Pearson Education Ltd.

Pekrun, R. (2006). The control-value theory of achievement emotions: Assumptions, corollaries, and implications for educational research and practice. *Educational Psychology Review, 18,* 315–341. https://doi.org/10.1007/s10648-006-9029-9

Pekrun, R., Lichtenfeld, S., Marsh, H.W., Murayama, K., & Goetz, T. (2017). Achievement emotions and academic performance: Longitudinal models of reciprocal effects. Child Development, 88, 1653–1670. https://doi.org/10.1111/cdev12704

Perryman, J., Ball, S., Maguire, M., & Braun, A. (2011). Life in the pressure cooker–School league tables and English and mathematics teachers' responses to accountability in a results-driven era. *British Journal of Educational Studies*, *59*(2), 179–195. https://doi.org/10.1080/00071005.2011.578568

Prasad, M. (2006). *The politics of free markets: The rise of neoliberal economic policies in Britain, France, Germany, and the United States.* University of Chicago Press.

Preiss, R.W., Gayle, B.M., & Allen, M. (2006). Test anxiety, academic self-efficacy, and study skills: A meta-analytic review. In B.M. Gayle, R.W. Preiss, & M. Allen (Eds.), *Classroom interaction and instructional processes: A meta-analytic review* (pp. 99–111). Lawrence Erlbaum Associates.

Putwain, D.W. (2007). Test Anxiety in UK schoolchildren: Prevalence and demographic patterns. *British Journal of Educational Psychology*, *77*(3), 579–593. https://doi.org/10.1348/000709906X161704

Putwain, D.W. (2008). Test anxiety and academic performance in KS4. *Educational Psychology in Practice*, *24*(4), 319–334. https://doi.org/10.1080/02667360802488765

Putwain, D.W. (2009). Assessment and examination stress in Key Stage 4. *British Educational Research Journal*, *35*(3), 391–411. https://doi.org/10.1080/01411920802044404

Putwain, D.W. (2019). An examination of the self-referent executive processing model of test anxiety: Control, emotional regulation, self-handicapping, and examination performance. *European Journal of Psychology of Education*, *34*(2), 341–358. https://doi.org/10.1007/s10212-018-0383-z

Putwain, D.W. (2020). *Examination pressures on children and young people: Are they taken seriously enough?* The British Academy.

Putwain, D.W., & Aveyard, B. (2018). Is perceived control a critical factor in understanding the negative relationship between cognitive test anxiety and examination performance? *School Psychology Quarterly*, *33*(1), 65–74. https://doi.org/10.1037/spq0000183

Putwain, D.W., Chamberlain, S., Daly, A., & Sadreddini, S. (2014). Reducing test anxiety among school-aged adolescents: A field experiment. *Educational Psychology in Practice*, *30*(4), 220–240. https://doi.org/10.1080/02667363.2014.964392

Putwain, D.W., Connors, L., & Symes, W. (2010). Do cognitive distortions mediate the test anxiety–examination performance relationship? *Educational Psychology*, *30*(1), 11–26. https://doi.org/10.1080/01443410903328866

Putwain, D.W., & Daly, A.L. (2014). Test anxiety prevalence and gender differences in a sample of English secondary school students. *Educational Studies*, *40*(5), 554–570. https://doi.org/10.1080/03055698.2014.953914

Putwain, D.W., Daly, A.L., Chamberlain, S., & Saddredini, S. (2016). "Sink or swim": Buoyancy and coping in the test anxiety and academic performance relationship. *Educational Psychology*, *36*(10), 1807–1825. https://doi.org/10.1080/01443410.2015.1066493

Putwain, D.W., Gallard, D.G., Beaumont, J., Loderer, K., & von der Embse, N. (2021). Does test anxiety predispose poor school-related wellbeing and enhanced risk of emotional disorders? *Cognitive Therapy and Research*, *45*(6), 1150–1163. https://doi.org/10.1007/s10608-021-10211-x

Putwain, D.W., Langdale, H.C., Woods, K.A., & Nicholson, L.J. (2011). Developing and piloting a dot-probe measure of attentional bias for test anxiety. *Learning and Individual Differences*, *21*(4), 478–482. https://doi.org/10.1016/j.lindif.2011.02.002

Putwain, D.W., Nicholson, L.J., Connors, E., & Woods, K.A. (2013). More resilient children are less test anxious and perform better in tests at the end of primary schooling. *Learning and Individual Differences*, *28*, 41–46. https://doi.org/10.1016/j.lindif.2013.09.010

Putwain, D.W., Pekrun, R., Rainbird, E.C., & Roberts, C.M. (2022). Cognitive-behavioural intervention for test anxiety: Could teachers deliver the STEPS program and what training would they require? In L.R.V. Gonzaga, L.L. Dellazzana-Zanon, & A.M.B. Silva (Eds.), *Handbook of stress and academic anxiety* (pp. 381–399). Springer. https://doi.org/10.1007/978-3-031-12737-3_25

Putwain, D.W., & Pescod, M. (2018). Is reducing uncertain control the key to successful test anxiety for secondary school students? Findings from a randomized control trial. *School Psychology Quarterly*, *33*(2), 283–292. https://doi.org/10.1037/spq0000228

Putwain, D.W., Stockinger, K., von der Embse, N.P., Suldo, S.M., & Daumiller, M. (2021). Test anxiety, anxiety disorders, and school-related wellbeing: Manifestations of the same or different constructs? *Journal of School Psychology*, *88*, 47–67. https://doi.org/10.1016/j.jsp.2021.08.001

Putwain, D.W., & Symes, W. (2018). Does increased effort compensate for performance debilitating test anxiety? *School Psychology Quarterly*, *33*(3), 482–491. https://doi.org/10.1037/spq0000236

Putwain, D.W., Symes, W., Connors, E., & Douglas-Osborn, E. (2012). Is academic buoyancy anything more than adaptive coping? *Anxiety, Stress and Coping*, *25*(3), 349–358. https://doi.org/10.1080/10615806.2011.582459

Putwain, D.W., Symes, W., Nicholson, L.J., & Remedios, R. (2021). Teacher motivational messages prior to examinations: What are they, how are they evaluated, and what are their educational outcomes? In A.J. Elliot (Ed.), *Advances in motivational science* (pp. 63–103). Academic Press. https://doi.org/10.1016/bs.adms.2020.01.001

Putwain, D.W., & von der Embse, N.P. (2021). Cognitive-behavioural intervention for test anxiety in adolescent students: Do benefits extend to school-related wellbeing and clinical anxiety. *Anxiety, Stress, and Coping*, *34*(1), 22–36. https://doi.org/10.1080/10615806.2020.1800656

Putwain, D.W., von der Embse, N.P., Rainbird, E.C., & West, G. (2021). The development and validation of a new multidimensional test anxiety scale (MTAS). *European Journal of Psychological Assessment*, *37*(3), 236–246. https://doi.org/10.1027/1015-5759/a000604

Putwain, D.W., Wood, P., & Pekrun, R. (2022). Achievement emotions and academic achievement: Reciprocal relations and the moderating influence of academic buoyancy. *Journal of Educational Psychology*, *114*(1), 108–126. https://doi.org/10.1037/edu0000637

Raban, S. (2008). *Examining the world: A history of the university of Cambridge local examinations syndicate.* Cambridge University Press.

Reay, D. (2010). Identity making in schools and classrooms. In M. Wheterell & C.T. Mohanty (Eds.), *The Sage handbook of identities* (pp. 277–294). Sage.

Richardson, M., Abraham, C., & Bond, R. (2012). Psychological correlates of university students' academic performance: A systematic review and meta-analysis. *Psychological Bulletin*, *138*(2), 353–387. https://doi.org/10.1037/a0026838

Robson, D.A., Johnstone, S.J., Putwain, D.W., & Howard, S. (2023). Test anxiety in primary school children: A 20-year systematic review and meta-analysis. *Journal of School Psychology*, 98, 39–60. https://doi.org/10.1016/j.jsp.2023.02.003

Rosenthal, R., & Rubin, D.B. (1982). A simple, general purpose display of magnitude of experimental effect. *Journal of Educational Psychology*, 74(2), 166–169. https://doi.org/10.1037/0022- 0663.74.2.166

Rowland, C.A. (2014). The effect of testing versus restudy on retention: A meta-analytic review of the testing effect. *Psychological Bulletin*, 140(6), 1432–1463. https://doi.org/10.1037/a0037559

Ryan, R.M., & Deci, E.L. (2001). On happiness and human potentials: A review of research on hedonic and eudaimonic well-being. *Annual Review of Psychology*, 52, 141–166. https://doi.org/10.1146/annurev.psych.52.1.141

Sawilowsky, S. (2009). New effect size rules of thumb. *Journal of Modern Applied Statistical Methods*, 8(2), 467–474. https://doi.org/10.22237/jmasm/1257035100

Schillinger, F.L., Mosbacher, J.A., Brunner, C., Vogel, S.E., & Grabner, R.H. (2021). Revisiting the role of worries in explaining the link between test anxiety and test performance. *Educational Psychology Review*, 33(4), 1887–1906. https://doi.org/10.1007/s10648-021-09601-0E

Schwinger, M., Trautner, M., Pütz, N., Fabianek, S., Lemmer, G., Lauermann, F., & Wirthwein, L. (2022). Why do students use strategies that hurt their chances of academic success? A meta-analysis of antecedents of academic self-handicapping. *Journal of Educational Psychology*, 114(3), 576–596. https://doi.org/10.1037/edu0000706

Seery, M.D. (2011). Challenge or threat? Cardiovascular indexes of resilience and vulnerability to potential stress in humans. *Neuroscience and Biobehavioral Reviews*, 35, 1603–1610. https://doi.org/10.1016/j.neubiorev.2011.03.00

Selkirk, L.C., Bouchey, H.A., & Eccles, J.S. (2011). Interactions among domain-specific expectancies, values, and gender: Predictors of test anxiety during early adolescence. *Journal of Early Adolescence*, 31(3), 361–389. https://doi.org/10.1177/0272431610363156

Senko, C., & Tropiano, K.L. (2016). Comparing three models of achievement goals: Goal orientations, goal standards, and goal complexes. *Journal of Educational Psychology*, 108(8), 1178–1192. https://doi.org/10.1037/edu0000114

Sireci, S.G. (2001). Standard setting using cluster analysis. In G.J. Cizek (Ed.), *Setting performance standards: Concepts, methods, and perspectives* (pp. 339–354). Lawrence Erlbaum.

Shafran, R., Myles-Hooton, P., Bennett, S., & Ost, L.G. (2021). The concept and definition of 'low intensity' cognitive behaviour therapy. *Behaviour Research and Therapy*, *138*, 103803. https://doi.org/10.1016/j.brat.2021.103803

Soares, D., & Woods, K. (2020). An international systematic literature review of test anxiety interventions 2011–2018. *Pastoral Care in Education*, *38*(4), 311–334, https://doi.org/10.1080/02643944.2020.1725909

Spada, M.M., Nikcevic, A.V., Moneta, G.B., & Ireson, J. (2006). Metacognition as a mediator of the effect of test anxiety on a surface approach to studying. *Educational Psychology*, *26*(5), 615–624. https://doi.org/10.1080/01443410500390673

Spielberger, C.D. (1966). Theory and research on anxiety. In C.D. Spielberger (Ed.), *Anxiety and behaviour* (pp. 3–20). Academic Press.

Spielberger, C.D. (1980). *Manual for test anxiety inventory*. Consulting Psychologists Press.

Steinmayr, R., Crede, J., McElvany, N., & Wirthwein, L. (2016). Subjective well-being, test anxiety, academic achievement: Testing for reciprocal effects. *Frontiers in Psychology*, *6*, 1994. https://doi.org/10.3389/fpsyg.2015.01994

Stöber, J. (2004). Dimensions of test anxiety: Relations to ways of coping with pre-exam anxiety and uncertainty. *Anxiety, Stress and Coping*, *17*(3), 213–226. https://doi.org/10.1080/10615800412331292615

Suldo, S.M., Thalji-Raitano, A., Kiefer, S.M., & Ferron, J.M. (2016). Conceptualizing high school students' mental health through a dual-factor model. *School Psychology Review*, *45*, 434–457. https://doi.org/10.17105/SPR45-4.434-457

Sung, Y.T., Chao, T.-Z., & Tseng, F.-L. (2016). Re-examining the relationship between test anxiety and learning achievement: An individual-differences perspective. *Contemporary Educational Psychology*, *46*, 241–252. https://doi.org/10.1016/j.cedpsych.2016.07.001

Thomas, C.L., Cassady, J.C., & Finch, W.H. (2018). Identifying severity standards on the cognitive test anxiety scale: Cut score determination using latent class and cluster analysis. *Journal of Psychoeducational Assessment*, *36*(5), 492–508. https://doi.org/10.1177/0734282916686004

Tomlinson, M. (2016). Students' perception of themselves as 'consumers' of higher education. *British Journal of Sociology of Education*, *38*(4), 450–467. https://doi.org/10.1080/01425692.2015.1113856

Travis, J., Kaszycki, A., Geden, M., & Bunde, J. (2020). Some stress is good stress: The challenge-hindrance framework, academic self-efficacy, and academic outcomes. *Journal of Educational Psychology, 112*, 1632–1643. https://doi.org/10.1037/edu0000478

Turner, B.G., Beidel, D.C., Hughes, S., & Turner, M.W. (1993). Text anxiety in African American school children. *School Psychology Quarterly*, *8*(2), 140–152. https://doi.org/10.1037/h0088835

Van Bockstaele, B., Verschuere, B., Tibboel, H., De Houwer, J., Crombez, G., & Koster, E.H.W. (2014). A review of current evidence for the causal impact of attentional bias on fear and anxiety. *Psychological Bulletin*, *140*(3), 682–721. https://doi.org/10.1037/a0034834

Vizard, T., Pearce, N., Davis, J., Sadler, K., Ford, T., Goodman, A., Goodman, R., & McManus, S. (2018). *Mental health of children and young people in England, 2017: Emotional disorders*. NHS Digital: Health and Social Care Information Centre.

von der Embse, N., Barterian, J., & Segool, N. (2013). Test anxiety interventions for children and adolescents: A systematic review of treatment studies from 2000–2010. *Psychology in the Schools*, *50*(1), 57–71. https://doi.org/10.1002/pits.21660

von der Embse, N., Jester, D., Roy, D., & Post, J. (2018). Test anxiety effects, predictors, and correlates: A 30-year meta-analytic review. *Journal of Affective Disorders*, *227*, 483–493. https://doi.org/10.1016/j.jad.2017.11.048

von der Embse, N.P., Putwain, D.W., & Francis, G. (2021). Interpretation and use of the Multidimensional Test Anxiety Scale (MTAS). *School Psychology*, *36*(2), 86–96. https://doi.org/10.1037/spq0000427

Walburg, V. (2014). Burnout among high school students: A literature review. *Children and Youth Services Review*, *42*, 28–33. https://doi.org/10.1016/j.childyouth.2014.03.020

Warren, M.K., Ollendick, T.H., & King, N.J. (1996). Test anxiety in girls and boys: A clinical-developmental analysis. *Behaviour Change*, *13*(3), 157–170. https://doi.org/10.1017/S0813483900004939

Weems, C.F., Scott, B.G., Taylor, L.K., Cannon, M.F., Romano, D.M., Perry, A.M., & Triplett, V. (2010). Test anxiety prevention and intervention programs in schools: Program development and rationale. *School Mental Health*, *2*, 62–71. https://doi.org/10.1007/s12310-010-9032-7

Wells, A. (2009). *Metacognitive therapy for anxiety and depression*. Guilford Press.

Wells, A., & Matthews, G. (1994). *Attention and emotion: A clinical perspective*. Lawrence Erlbaum Associates.

Wells, A., & Matthews, G. (1996). Modelling cognition in emotional disorder: The S-REF model. *Behaviour Research and Therapy*, *34*, 881–888. https://doi.org/10.1016/S0005-7967(96)00050-2

Williams, C., & Chellingsworth, M. (2010). *CBT: A clinicians guide to using the five areas approach*. Hodder Arnold.

World Health Organization. (2018). International classification of diseases for mortality and morbidity statistics (11th Edition). World Health organization.

Yale-Soulière, G., Campeau, G., Turgeon, L., & Goulet, J. (2024). Evaluation of a brief intervention to reduce test anxiety in adolescents: A randomized control trial. Manuscript under review.

Yale-Soulière, G., Morizot, J., Belcher, J., & Wuthrich, V. (2024). Understanding the hierarchical factor structure of anxiety symptoms in an adolescent sample and its relationship to depression. Manuscript under review.

Yeager, D.S., & Dweck, C.S. (2020). What can be learned from growth mindset controversies? *American Psychologist*, *75*(9), 1269–1284. https://doi.org/10.1037/amp0000794

Yerkes, R.M., & Dodson, J.D. (1908). The relation of strength of stimulus to rapidity of habit-formation. *Journal of Comparative Neurology and Psychology*, *18*(5), 459–482. https://doi.org/10.1002/cne.920180503

Zeidner, M. (1994). Personal and contextual determinants of coping and anxiety in an evaluative situation: A prospective study. *Personality and Individual Differences*, *16*(6), 899–918. https://doi.org/10.1016/0191-8869(94)90234-8

Zeidner, M. (1995). Adaptive coping with test situations: A review of the literature. *Educational Psychologist*, *30*(3), 123–133. https://doi.org/10.1207/s15326985ep3003_3

Zeidner, M. (1996). How do high school and college students cope with test situations? *British Journal of Educational Psychology*, *66*(1), 115–128. https://doi.org/10.1111/j.2044-8279.1996.tb01181.x

Zeidner, M., & Matthews, G. (2005). Evaluation anxiety. In A.J. Elliot & C.S. Dweck (Eds.), *Handbook of competence and motivation* (pp. 141–163). Guilford Press.

Zimmer, J.W., & Hocevar, D.J. (1994). Effects of massed versus distributed practice of test taking on achievement and test anxiety. *Psychological Reports*, 74(3), 915–919. https://doi.org/10.2466/pr0.1994.74.3.915